CW01019976

A CANNY LAD

The author at Peterhouse, Cambridge

A CANNY LAD

The early life of Thomas Moffett

AN AUTOBIOGRAPHY

ERSKINE PRESS

1998

First published in 1998 by
The Erskine Press, The Old Bakery, Banham, Norfolk

©Thomas Moffett, 1998

ISBN 1 85297 052 9

British Library Cataloguing in Publication Data
A catalogue record of this book is available
from the British Library

Printed in England

This book is dedicated to the memory of my mother, Mary Ann Spoors Moffett 1904–31; of my wife, Lillian Moffett, 1921–93; of Professor Edward Shils 1910–94; and to my sons, Mark and John.

CONTENTS

List of Illustrations   viii

Foreword   ix

Introduction   xi
   by Professor Sir Henry Chadwick KBE

Part I: Early Days   1

Part II: 'We are the Orphanage Boys!'   69

Epilogue   129

LIST OF ILLUSTRATIONS

The author at Peterhouse, Cambridge	*Frontispiece*
1. Wapping Street about 1888	2
2. Thrift Street in 1898	3
3. Comical Corner and the ferry landing	4
4. The South End of Long Row	5
5. The tug *Washington* off Broad Landing	6
6. William, Mary and George in 1930	14
7. Lower Thames Street in 1910	17
8. The lifeboat *Bedford*	24
9. The Palatine Hotel in 1920	26
10. My mother	34
11. Views of 25/27 Ladies Walk	36
12. Family group	58
13. Asylum for Thoroughly Destitute Children	70
14. Title page of the prospectus	72
15. The giant sequoia planted by Queen Victoria	75
16. The back of the Royal Albert Orphanage	76/77
17. Nurse Eileen and Miss Williams	79
18. Boys on the fire escape	83
19. The staff	87
20. The tailor's shop	90
21. Practising for sports day	95
22. Miss Mueller's morris dancers	98
23. Myself with billiard cue and friends	100
24. The carpenter's shop	112
25. Old Boys	128
26. William in the Navy	131

FOREWORD

I was persuaded to write down the story of my childhood by two people: my second wife, Lillian, and my friend, Professor Edward Shils. They convinced me I had a tale to tell, and bullied me to keep at it. My reason for doing it was to give my children, and their children, a glimpse of their family history, and some idea of what life was like in the 1920s and 30s. Then one or two people read the manuscript, and said they thought I had the makings of a book, a small personal record, for those interested in social history.

The years I describe were hard, and my brothers and I suffered pain and deprivation, but there were good times and compassionate people too, and I write with no feelings of bitterness or self-pity.

This is not a-rags-to-riches story in any material sense. In the early days the rags were real enough, but the riches I acquired were my contacts and friendships with an incredibly varied range of people. I gradually learnt to accept life as it comes, and to realise that when one door closes another will probably open.

Revising my manuscript has brought home to me how strangely memory works. There are large important gaps that I cannot fill, yet odd, trivial details – a car registration number, a brand name, for example – remain printed indelibly on my mind.

My thanks are due to the South Tyneside Metropolitan Borough Council who supplied the photographs for figures 1–5, 7–9 and 11, and kindly agreed to waive their copyright fee.

Finally, I should like to thank Dr Carmen Blacker and Dr Michael Loewe for their advice and encouragement, and, above all, Julia Manheim, who edited the text and prepared it for publication.

Cambridge, January 1998   THOMAS MOFFETT

INTRODUCTION

by Professor Sir Henry Chadwick KBE

In 1987, a surprise invitation from the governing body of Peterhouse, Cambridge, to succeed Lord Dacre in the office of Master, brought six years of friendship and daily co-operation with Tom Moffett, ended only by statutory retirement from the Mastership and a move away from Cambridge. For some time past, Tom had been college butler, a front man in caring for the fellows, and very prominent on large public occasions. In the course of my first year he reached the retiring age, but since he was as active as ever, at my request he was invited to move to the Master's lodge, where his rocklike integrity became one of the grand immovables. He knew how things should be done. During his years at Peterhouse he had won the hearts and admiration of the fellows, who were delighted to realise that, though retired from looking after them, his migration across Trumpington Street to Queen Anne Lodge ensured a continuing capacity to help the college on important occasions when he was needed. Moreover, at the Master's lodge graduates and undergraduates coming in for a meal would be received with a simple courtesy and direct dignity which graced the house.

This memoir of early, stormy years provides a vivid picture of times and social customs not readily recalled today, and of the rough, often inhuman manner in which, even within living memory, vulnerable children, and especially orphans, might be disgracefully treated by people in positions of responsibility, who ought to have known and done much better. During the Second World War, Tom served in the Navy in dangerous places. His years in Cambridge, especially at Peterhouse, became like an Indian summer. When, very sadly, his wife Lillian died, there was a testimony to the deep respect and affection in which they were both held that at the funeral the Church of Little St Mary's was full to overflowing, and the congregation, mainly from the college, sang with feeling for him and the family 'The old rugged cross' as a Northumbrian would. Important in the life of the College generally was a special relationship that he developed with the eminent American professor of social studies, Edward Shils, who used to spend some months each year at Peterhouse. When for Ed Shils death began to approach in Chicago, Tom was the man to fly the Atlantic to look after him and to provide comfort and care during his last days.

PART I

Early Days

Fig 1. *It was a very desolate place.*

I can still conjure up a distinct picture of the part of South Shields where I spent the first eight or so years of my life. It was a very desolate place. A long curving road – called successively Thrift Street, Long Row, Wapping Street, and Shadwell Street – ran parallel with the river Tyne on its south bank between the market place and the groyne, built like a snout sticking out into the river to stop the drifting of the beach and check the encroachment of the North Sea.

On the river side was a grimy redbrick wall some fourteen feet high – higher in places where tall buildings backed directly on to the street. This was the outer wall of the docks,

Fig 2. *A long curving road called Thrift Street.*

Fig 3. *A short street called Comical Corner, leading to the landing stage for one of the ferries.*

and inside it were to be found ship-repair yards, graving yards, various marine and engineering enterprises, towering cranes, and black menacing warehouses. Here and there, a gap in the wall gave access to the river via a flight of steps, or a sort of cobbled beach. One such gave on to Coble Landing, the slipway of the Tyne lifeboat, another on to the Trinity House building from which the pilots used to go out to the ships in the river.

The steps were also used by the foreboatmen, owners of small scullers, who worked with the tugboats helping to moor the ocean-going ships. Their job was to gather the lines from the ships and secure them to a buoy or jetty whilst the tugs manoeuvred the vessel into position. They rowed up and down the river, or sometimes hitched a tow, by attaching their boathook to the stern of a tug, in order to be near at hand whenever they were needed.

Fig 4. *We lived first in Long Row, in an area called the Stanhope.*

Fig 5. *When the tide was right, we kids were able to scramble round the piles of the jetty and play at running across the timber.*

On the town side the land rose steeply, and in many places the streets running down towards the river ended in a flight of steps. There were Dog Lowp Stairs, for example, said to be haunted. A short street called Comical Corner, leading to the landing stage for one of the ferries, was celebrated by a local author in a play called *The Angel of Comical Corner*, which was performed at the Alexandra Theatre in the town.

We lived first in Long Row, in an area called the Stanhope. It was originally known as the Stanhope Drops, a name that goes back to the days of sail. The collier brigs used to load their cargoes at this point, and after they had discharged their ballast, the coal was poured down chutes into their holds: hence the name the Drops. The ballast accumulated to form large hills upon which tenement houses were built, and we later moved to a house on Ballast Hill.

Naturally, there was a public house close by, the Stanhope Hotel, and in front of its door, in all weathers, stood Blind Geordie. He had been blind from birth, but his hearing was so acute that he could tell from the sound of the footsteps which of his many friends or acquaintances was arriving.

A little further along the street was Wardle's Sawmill, and at Broad Landing huge rafts of timber floated on the river. When the tide was right, we kids were able to scramble round the piles of the jetty and play at running across the timber. The slippery logs spun and bobbed beneath our bare scampering feet, and it is surprising there were so few mishaps. The river police would try to chase us off, but we always returned to dare one another to more and more dangerous escapades. I did hear of a boy who slipped and went under the raft; and his body was not recovered for some days.

At the top of Thrift Street was the market place, and in the winter months after dark each stall was lit by flaring paraffin lamps. Here Toffee Randall made and sold his wares, entrancing and entertaining his customers as he pulled hot toffee with steel hooks, stretching and mixing different colours to produce striped toffee and humbugs.

A character called Pip Squeak had a special technique for selling chocolate. He'd fill a bag with bars of chocolate and other sweetmeats, then appear to drop a two-shilling piece into the bag and offer it all for half a crown. Needless to say, when you got the bag home there'd be no two-shilling piece in it.

The butchers' stalls did a roaring trade as closing time approached, particularly on a Saturday night, for they sold off their meat cheaply. A lot of women used to go along as late as possible, hoping to pick up the weekly joint for about a shilling or one and sixpence.

Two ferries plied the Tyne to North Shields; one from a point about a hundred and fifty yards from the groyne, and the other from a landing stage just off the market place. The former was used by pedestrian passengers only and the fare was one penny for one way, children half price, and it was known as the Ha'penny Dodger. The latter took both pedestrians and vehicles, and the fare was two pence, for the journey was a little longer. Of those fortunate enough to have work in North Shields, most used the Ha'penny Dodger, and then walked along Wapping Street, through Long Row to the market place to catch the train or bus home.

At the top of this landing stage, where the sailing ships moored and the foreboatmen came ashore, was a hostelry called the Alum House Ham. Its name comes from a chemical works, set up to produce alum for glass-making in the late seventeenth and early eighteenth century. It is there to this day and is celebrated in the following lines:

> The ships lay off Alum House Ham
> > Awaiting the wind the tide.
> The *Brotherly Love*, the *Amphitrite*,
> And the *Betsy Cairns*, so stout and tight,
> > All floated side by side.

This part of South Shields was home to the unemployed, the down-and-outs, the undeserving poor, and the people who came from here were known as Skyetenders. This name was originally given to those who lived near Salmon's Quay, the place where fishermen used to lay out their catch before the fish quay at North Shields was built. In those days skate was plentiful and cheap, and the Salmon Quay area became known at the skate end, or skyet end.

*   *   *

The building in which I spent the earliest part of my life was, as I have said, in Long Row. On the south side towards the market place, a long triangle of waste ground sloped up to the street above and, just before the point where the two streets converged, and opposite a particularly high stretch of wall, stood a row of terrace houses. In fact, the facades looked more like a wall than houses; just a few squares were cut out to make windows, and the front doors opened straight on to the street. Whole families occupied either a ground floor or an upper floor, or sometimes, as in our case, a single room; and those at the back of the building had to traverse a long, dark, narrow passageway in order to enter their quarters.

We were on the ground floor. My mother, father, two

younger brothers, younger sister and I lived in a room about fifteen foot square. It was sparsely furnished with a table and four wooden chairs, a double bed for my parents, and a wardrobe-type bed for us children, in which we slept two-and-two, head-to-toe. A coal-burning, iron cooking range had an oven on one side and a fire grate on the other, and it heated the water. No ray of sunlight ever penetrated our home.

Some of my earliest memories are of playing on one of the flights of steps that led down to the river as I waited for my father to return from work on the ferry. Near its mouth, the Tyne is strongly tidal, and at full flood these steps were completely covered; but at low tide it was possible to walk on the mud of the riverbed and scramble about amongst the jetsam, and the faeces discharged from a nearby sewer. Many a time I'd hear Da call out, 'Tom! Haven't I told you to keep away from those steps?' And the blows would rain down on my head. I realise now that he was not being cruel; this was simply his way of showing concern for my safety, for it was a dangerous place. Wave-traps stuck out into the river, and when the tide was flowing the brown swirling water was full of eddies.

My father would also chastise me for accosting people who had come off the ferry: 'Got any bait, mister? Have you got any bait?' (Bait is an obsolete word, except in Geordie, that originally meant food in general; but by the middle of the nineteenth century it had come to mean the provisions Northumberland and Durham miners took to work.) Often I'd be lucky and get a bite to eat, perhaps a sandwich left over from someone's lunch, but often too Da would box my ears. 'Don't let me ever catch you doing such a thing again.' He had his pride; this was begging, and, no matter how little we had, how poor and hungry we were, begging was degrading.

Respectability was very important to most poor families. They did not want others to look down on them and so took great pains to appear above reproach, especially as far as the police and the law were concerned. If a youngster was caught at some misdemeanour, he would far rather the local policeman cuffed him and sent him on his way with a sore ear and a tear in his eye, than took his name and address and reported him to his parents.

*   *   *

My father, whose names were William Gray Moffett, was, as I remember him, a very handsome man with blond wavy hair, and he stood about five foot eight or nine inches. I'd always believed he was a stone mason, like his father before him, but he was a plasterer by trade, and, so I've been told, a very good one. This probably explains why he never seemed to have any trouble obtaining work at a time of high unemployment. He was also intelligent and knew how to present himself, and for a time he was employed in North Shields. I feel very strongly that if he hadn't spent so much money on drink, and treating his so-called friends – who, incidentally thought he was a great guy – I wouldn't have been so hungry, and wouldn't have had to resort to begging for bait. Nor would my poor mother, in the few years she was alive during my childhood, have had such a hard time trying to keep us fed and clad.

I am afraid, however, that this was very much the accepted pattern of life in my young days; no matter how little work or money the menfolk had, they never went without their pint of beer, or, in my father's case, tot of whisky. He never drank beer; as far as he was concerned, it was a waste of money. If he

11

offered to buy you a drink and you asked for a beer, you could buy your own; if you asked for spirits he would treat you.

I have been given to understand by an aunt, my mother's sister, that my father would beat my mother when he came home drunk – and I shall never forgive him for this. I know little about his drinking friends; most of them, I believe, were chaps he had grown up with, or with whom he had been through the Great War.

In addition to his fondness for alcohol, I am informed by people who knew him that my father was something of a womanizer. One lady I knew quite well recalled walking along the street with my mother, who was pushing a perambulator containing three children, when they saw him on the opposite side arm in arm with another woman. This, apparently, led to a fierce row between my parents when my father came home that night. Thus, I can only assume that he spent some of his wages on other women.

I never recall my father staying in of an evening, or at any other time, for that matter. After finishing his evening meal, he would dress up and go down to the Scotia Bar. He was always very smartly turned out. So too were most of the menfolk in that part of the country; all of them seemed to have a decent suit of clothes – sometimes a little threadbare perhaps – to go out in at the weekend. They looked after these garments and, when the weekend was over, they would almost invariably go back into pawn till the following Friday, when their wives would have to redeem them in time for the weekend. And so it went on.

Once my father had changed after his meal and gone out, my mother, poor soul, would be left behind with us children. She, as I fondly remember, was a rather rotund, demure and inoffensive person. She had jet-black hair, and was only about five foot tall. Her names were Mary Ann Spoors Moffett.

I was the eldest of her children, born in 1923. My brother William Gray came along fourteen months later, and George followed him in 1926. After a gap of three years, my sister Mary Ann Spoors Telford was born, and Eva was born in 1930. I can remember Ma having to keep us quiet within the confines of that single, sunless room when William was lying dangerously ill. He had diphtheria and was eventually taken off to hospital in an ambulance, with all the neighbours hovering around in morbid curiosity. In those pre-inoculation days diphtheria was a major killer, and William was lucky to survive.

*   *   *

Shortly after William's recovery we moved to another tenement: 5 Studley Stairs, off Lower Thames Street. Why we moved I don't know; I suppose my parents wanted a larger place. As I have said, the ground rose very steeply up from the river; Lower Thames Street ran more or less parallel to Long Row, and from our new house we looked down on the roof of the building we had just left. The houses in this street seemed to sit on a sort of ledge cut out of the side of Ballast Hill. Studley Stairs, a flight of concrete steps, took you to the top of the hill, from which there was a view of the railway station and turntable, and this was a grand place to play.

Once again, we were on the ground floor, but the great difference between our new and old quarters was that we now had a view of the river over the tops of the wharves and warehouses. From our window we could see the ferries crossing the Tyne and watch the movement of shipping. Best of all, we had plenty of natural light.

Fig 6. *My brother William Gray came along in 1925, and George followed him in 1926. After a gap of three years my sister Mary Ann Spoors Telford was born.*

We also moved from one room to two. The main one was L-shaped, with a fireplace and oven, and the second, leading off it, was under the staircase that led to the flat above, occupied by an old lady and her grown-up son.

My parents slept in the smaller room with the baby, and my sister, two brothers and I continued to share a bed in the living room. The privy was across the yard outside, as was the tap that supplied all our water. We drew water for drinking and cooking and kept it inside in an enamel pail, and in the night we all urinated into a galvanised bucket.

Our few sticks of furniture came with us from Long Row pushed in a handcart. Every family had a handcart in those days, and I'm sure the neighbours would have helped with the move. Our wardrobe bed, I remember, took in half. The floor of the new place was covered with linoleum and there was a hooky mat in front of the fire. Hooky mats were made from narrow strips of rag cut into lengths of about three inches and pushed with a peg into a square of hessian. People made their own from whatever bits and pieces they had available, and they could be pretty and colourful.

Ma's few ornaments stood on the mantelpiece. One night, after my father had been drinking, he returned home and an argument broke out between my parents. He seized a silver-headed malacca cane, which had belonged to his father, and swept everything off the mantelpiece. He then came over to the bed, where we were cowering under the covers, and whacked the cane down first on one side then on the other, ignoring Ma's screams for him to stop.

Times were hard, and we were often hungry. I simply do not know how my mother fed her large family. I would say that our staple diet was bread and margarine, but we did also get stew made from very cheap scraps of meat, eked out with dumplings or potatoes. On rare occasions there would be a little bacon for Sunday breakfast, but I never remember having a solid piece of meat or a chicken – not even at Christmas. Also, I can't recall sitting down to a meal with my parents; most of the time I'd take my piece of bread and whatever out with me, and eat it while I was playing.

Ma cooked on the open coal fire which was kept alight at all times; the blackened kettle used to sing quietly in the background, its water just off the boil. She had a frying pan, an iron saucepan, and an oval iron mormis, or cauldron boiler, with a handle across the top. She made our bread, baking it in the oven at the side of the range which was heated by pushing the hot coals from the fire underneath it.

The entire family's clothes were kept in one small chest of drawers. Speaking for myself, I think I had two shirts, two pairs of short trousers, and a jersey for best, for going to Sunday school. I had no socks, and only occasionally a pair of boots or shoes. Underclothing I never even knew existed, and I didn't possess a pair of pyjamas. We slept in the shirts we had been wearing during the day, and ran about the streets and went to school barefoot.

Our neighbours were a rather rough lot, for in those times of poverty it was a struggle to survive; yet people had enough compassion to come to one another's aid, and I think they helped my mother quite a bit. The old lady upstairs may have been somewhat mentally deranged; we children were certainly scared of her. She had been asked to keep an ear open for us one night after we were supposed to be in bed, but we were not inclined to sleep and were making quite a racket. Down she came, holding a large black umbrella over her

Fig 7. *Why we moved I don't know; I suppose my parents wanted a larger place.*

head, and walked up and down the room. Was she trying to frighten us to sleep, I wonder? Whatever she thought she was doing, we certainly quietened right down and she never heard another peep out of us.

* * *

Whilst we were living on Studley Stairs my father suddenly disappeared. I wasn't told the reason for this. Then, after a while, he started coming home at weekends, and I later learned that he was being treated for tuberculosis in the sanatorium. In addition to his TB he had trench fever, a disease transmitted by the bite of a body louse, that ran riot amongst the soldiers of the Great War. After his death, my grandmother told me he'd had a bullet near his brain, and a plate inserted in his skull to prevent its dislodging. He'd also been hit in the chest by a bullet, but this one had been removed and was on show on Ganny's mantelpiece.

My father never spoke to me, or to any of us children, about his wartime experiences. But I do know that he said repeatedly that he would never allow any of us to join the services, or to go down the mines.

This must have been a very, very hard time for my mother, as she herself was already ill. In fact, she could have left my father a while since, as I am told an aunt of hers wanted her to go and live with her; but she would never do so, and I can only think it was for our sakes as she would have had to put us in an orphanage. Instead, she tried heroically to keep us all together as a family, putting up with my father's drinking and his violence, feeding and clothing us on almost no money.

My sister Eva was born whilst we lived on Studley Stairs. I can recall little about her except that I had to mind her quite a bit as Ma was no longer able to cope; but one incident I do remember. In those days almost every street had its corner shop that sold anything and everything: safety pins, candles, mouse traps, bacon, and biscuits which you selected from large tins, or bought cheap if they were broken. Eva was teething and fractious, so Ma sent me down to the shop with her to buy a ha'penny bar of chocolate for her to suck. On the way home she obviously dropped it, and, as she was looking over my shoulder, I never noticed. When we got home there was no chocolate to show, the baby was howling, and Ma accused me of eating it myself. This was the sort of thing I might well have done, for I was no angel, but I hadn't, and the accusation rankles to this day. She tried to box my ears, but I skipped out of her way, and she was no longer quick enough to catch me.

Soon after this incident Eva died of teething problems, bronchitis, and diarrhoea, a mere seven months old. William and I attended her funeral, and walked in the silent procession up and over Long Bank and down the cobbled streets to Saint Stephen's Church. My father's four surviving brothers, Harry, Tommy, Foster, and Alex, were there, and two of them carried the tiny white coffin with brass handles. I don't think Da himself was there; he must have been in the sanatorium. I am assuming there was no money for a hearse, and there were no flowers. Eva is buried in the churchyard. My mother did not attend the funeral either, as she was too ill. She stayed at home with George and Mary, who were too young to go.

*   *   *

Up till now there had been seven of us living in the two rooms; suddenly there were six. This was the beginning of the breakup of my family. I shall never know what my poor mother must have been going through at this time. She had just lost a baby, she had four children under the age of seven, her husband was being treated for tuberculosis, and her own health and strength were fast ebbing away.

With my father absent during the week, Ma had to carry our water supply and our coal in from the yard, and empty the galvanised bucket. I was supposed to share these tasks, but I was not as conscientious or thoughtful as I should have been – if only one could realise one's thoughtlessness in time to do something about it. All this was before the creation of the welfare state, and I have no idea where the money came from; I assume my parents must have contributed to some kind of insurance scheme.

I'd started attending Saint Stephen's National School by now. It had opened around 1863 and provided for 600 boys and girls; the young children and the older ones were taught in different buildings, separated by a high wall. We lived two-and-a-half miles away, and I walked there and back twice a day, for this was before the days of school dinners. Lessons began at 9 o'clock and I'd leave home in the morning with a slice of bread and margarine, which I ate on the way. It was pleasant enough in the summer, for my route took me past the railway station, and I loved watching the engines being moved around on the turntable, but winter was another matter. My toes would be like little icicles and I had chronic chilblains. Poor dear Ma would come and meet me halfway; and, although I'd vow to be brave as I set out for home in the vicious North East wind that blew in off the sea, invariably, by the time I caught sight of her, I would be sobbing from the cold. She would wrap my hands in her apron to try to warm them. She herself can't have been so very warm, for I don't recall her wearing a coat or shawl, and perhaps she'd have only a pair of slippers on her feet, but to me she was warmth itself. I have always said to my own children, and to any apprentice boys who have been in my care, 'Remember, you will only have one mother in this world.'

I may have given the impression that my young life was one of unrelieved misery and deprivation, but this was not so. One morning, soon after I started school, a policeman came into our classroom. Needless to say, I imagined he'd come looking for me, though I did notice that some of my fellow pupils had also fallen unnaturally silent and were busy assuming an air of injured innocence. However, he did not seem interested in us, and after some words with our teacher, he asked all the children who had no shoes to leave their desks and come to the front of the room. Quite a few of us came forward, and he handed each of us a ticket to take home to our parents, which they could exchange for a pair of boots. What a red-letter day this was! The Police Federation had collected this money, and the memory of this humane gesture has left me with a lasting respect for the police of this country.

Nor was my father without his kinder side. I can remember him coming home one weekend and pulling a torch out of his pocket. 'Would you like Father Christmas to bring you a torch like this? Or would you like a flat one?' he asked. I looked at the torch he was holding; it was some five inches long, about one-and-a-half in diameter, and had a big bulbous glass top. 'I'd like one like this.' And in my stocking on Christmas morning there was a torch with a bulbous top, an apple, an orange, and a penny bar of chocolate. All day long I switched that torch on and off, with the result that by the evening the battery was spent, and I cried when my torch would not shine in the dark.

* * *

Despite the trials and tribulations of poverty, the ravages made upon my family by the demon drink, and the all-too-visible signs of destitution around us, we children did manage to have a lot of fun, largely, I think, because our entertainments were simple and we created most of them ourselves. There was, of course, no television, and families with a wireless set were few and far between. Obviously, there were people who could afford to go to the cinema, but I seldom had the wherewithal to get into the 'penny rush', a Saturday-morning show at the local picture house.

We were all keen collectors of cigarette cards, which, perhaps I should explain for those too young to remember such things, used to come in cigarette packets. There were some very good sets: film stars, wild animals, railway engines, cricketers, footballers, and ships. There were also miniature silk flags, the size of the cards, that you could save up and send in to be exchanged for a full-size flag. I recall one Saturday evening, when I should have stayed at home with Ma, I went out looking for cards in the busiest part of town, right alongside the river and the docks, and I lost all sense of time. Pardonable offenses, perhaps, but I know that I should not have been going up to men in the street and asking for cards. Once or twice I got the threat of a 'byeut i' the hintend' – a boot up the behind – but most people were decent enough to open up the packet and give me the card. In the meantime, my father returned from the sanatorium, found Ma at her wits' end with worry, and immediately set out to look for me. He caught me red-handed, boxed my ears, grabbed me by the scruff of the neck and marched me home. It was past eleven o'clock, and it says something for those far-off days that a seven-year-old kid could wander around a rough city like South Shields importuning strangers late at night and come to no harm.

We all used to play in the street, and when darkness fell early, we would wait impatiently for the colley, or lamplighter, to come by with his long pole which he hooked into the chain that hung beside the pilot light in the gas lamps. We'd see the lights come on as he worked his way up the street, and would stop whatever we were up to and chorus:

> Colley wiv a lamp,
> Colley wiv a leet,
> Colley wiv a little dog barkin' at his feet.

One of the games we played involved our cigarette cards. You propped one up against a wall, then, from a distance of about eight feet away flicked another card at it, the aim being to knock it down. We took turns flicking and the first person to knock down the standing card claimed it and all the others that had been flicked, but left behind his last card to start the next round.

'All the bairns haz gatten a gord ti play wi'.' Gords were steel hoops – wooden ones were too light – and we could really make those gords move. We guided them with slender iron rods that ended in a hook, and this made them very manoeuvrable, as we could pick them up and twirl them above our heads, toss them and catch them, and do all manner of tricks. We bowled them all over the place; even if we were sent on an errand – or message as it is always called in the

Fig 8. *So the lifeboat was named the* Bedford.

North – as long as there was not a lot to be carried, we'd take the gord with us.

Nearly all my friends had a whip and top, handed down through the family, I suppose, as mine were. We played football with old tin cans, or clootie baals, balls made of rags bound up with string. At the time of local elections we attacked one another with baster baals, balls made of tightly scrunched up paper swung on the end of a length of string. Kids whose parents favoured one candidate would bash those whose parents voted another way.

Hitchy dabber was a form of hopscotch, and everys a street version of hunt the thimble. We'd scrounge some object from a market-stall holder, a bit of bruised fruit, or some broken bits from a toffee tray, say, and one person would hide it, while we covered our eyes and counted up to fifty. When it was found, the finder shouted 'Everys!' so we could gather round and share it. Montakity was played in teams, boys and girls together, with sometimes as many as eighteen or twenty joining in. The members of one team would stand in a line and bend over, the head of the person behind between the legs of the one in front, with the front person of all leaning up against a wall to brace the whole line. Then members of second team would make a series of flying jumps to mount the backs of the first; those in the front had to get far enough along the bent backs to leave room for those bringing up the rear. When everyone had jumped, you counted one, two, three, and if the benders collapsed before the count was up, they had to bend down again until they managed to hold up. And so it went on, till we all collapsed in a heap.

One of my cousins, who was blind, used to join in all our games and could always be found in the thick of things. I thought he was really clever; he played by ear and showed no fear of the rough and tumble. For my part, I was always a bit of a loner, and would go off and spend time down by the river, or on the beach. There was a place on the river called the Coble – a coble is a flat-bottomed fishing boat – where the lifeboat was housed, and I loved watching the lifeboatmen working on their boat keeping it ship-shape for any emergency. The lifeboat had been built with money donated by a Miss Bedford, in memory of her brother, who had been an engineer with the Tyne Improvement Commission, so the lifeboat was named the *Bedford*.

Down on the beach the first place I'd make for was the groyne. There were usually two or three men standing on it, casting their lines into the sea, and sometimes they'd ask me to dig crabs for them to bait their hooks with. I loved watching the ships passing into and out of the river; the funnel markings

Fig 9. Once more we were on the move ... perhaps my father wanted to be nearer one of his favourite haunts, a pub called the Palatine.

showed which line a ship belonged to, and I grew quite good at recognising these. The beach itself had beautiful fine sand, no rocks or pebbles, and the part I liked best was a strip, about half a mile long, between the groyne and the pier, which was actually in the river mouth. It was usually referred to as the North Beach, though its real name was Herd Sands. The beach on the other side of the pier, known as the South Beach, stretched for miles, past Marsden Rock, now a bird sanctuary, and almost to the town of Sunderland. They were both beautiful clean beaches, the finest on the east coast of England, so I have always thought – but then I may be prejudiced.

*   *   *

Once more we were on the move, further up the hill, in fact this time right to the top. I always thought it was the rich who moved upwards, but as far as I could see no more money had come our way. We had only lived in the other place about six months; perhaps my father wanted to be nearer one of his favourite haunts, a pub called the Palatine, though he was still spending most of his time in the sanatorium.

Again, we were in a two-room flat in a small tenement. The quarters were rather smaller than those we had left, but more compact and homely. The building stood on a sort of concrete plateau, which was surrounded by iron railings and accessible only by a flight of concrete steps at either end. This was Heugh Street – heugh in Geordie means a precipitous hill or cliff.

From our new place we had a glorious view of the river; we could follow its course from the bend at Tyne Dock right to its mouth. And beyond that lay the open sea. There was always something of interest going on: the trawler fleet coming and going, the ferries and tugs plying to and fro. Just up river from the trawler jetty was moored a large Royal Navy ship, the *Wellesley*. This was said to be a training vessel, but rumour had it that it was a RN detention ship. Across the river were North Shields and Tynemouth, and then you could see the hills of Northumberland. This must be some of the most beautiful country in the British Isles, but oh, those bitter easterly winds!

On the one hand, I was quite happy about our move because it brought me nearer to my school. I just had to negotiate the steps one end of the terrace, go down the Palatine Bank, and I was almost at the school gates. If I went down the steps at the other end, and followed the road round, a route that wasn't much further, I had to pass the tenement where Ganny Moffett lived. I never took this way as I didn't want Ganny seeing what mischief I got up to and reporting it to my Da.

The main drawback to our new abode was that directly beneath us was the flat occupied by an uncle, aunt and cousin, and we were constantly being told to make less noise. It was a bit of a trial for all concerned: there were four of us children, three boys under the age of seven and little Mary, who was still a baby; and Ma, sick and exhausted, had to cope with us single-handed most of the time. These Moffett relatives – the aunt was my father's sister – always seemed rather aloof and unsympathetic; I had the impression they considered themselves a cut above us. I don't know what my uncle did for a living; I don't ever recall seeing him go to work. Perhaps, like so many men at that time, he was unemployed.

None of this concerned me unduly, for I was having as much fun as ever, and the challenge of keeping one jump ahead of my relatives kept me on my toes. My head was full of fantasies. I still hung around the ferry terminal and the lifeboat station. I loved watching the pilot boats going about their duties, and the police launches racing up and down the river. I longed to be aboard one of them. I imagined myself a seaman on an ocean-going liner, travelling all over the world. I saw myself with lots of money to spend, because when the sailors came ashore they always seemed to have pockets full of money. Right through my teens I nursed this earnest desire to join the Navy.

Another place where I spent a good deal of time was at the funeral depository, down the bank in one of the cross streets, about three minutes' walk away. There were stables around the back, and the hearses and carriages were kept in a corner of the yard. Many an hour I spent watching the men polishing harness, and grooming the beautiful black horses till their coats shone. To my young eyes a funeral cortege was one of the most majestic sights in the world.

At the very bottom of the bank, a hundred and fifty yards further on, was a small fish smokery. The skilful employees worked at lightning speed gutting and splitting the herrings, then threading them on poles to hang over the smoking oak chips that turned them into kippers or bloaters. How vividly I can recall the glorious smell of that little factory. If I got under the men's feet I was told to clear off, but when this happened I was usually given a pair of kippers to take home.

I'd go scrounging around the coal merchants' yards, collecting bits of coal that had fallen off the barrows and wagons. I even climbed over the wall into the railway turntable enclosure to pick up the lumps that had fallen off the engine tender. This rather dangerous area offered rich pickings, and the coal I brought home kept the fire alight when we could not afford to buy fuel. I also scoured the beach for driftwood. I have to admit, though, that I wasn't always such a good and resourceful boy as these actions might imply, nor was I as obedient as I should have been. Ma would have been horrified had she known half the things I got up to.

I didn't go off on my own all the time. A whole crowd of us used to go around together, though I should emphasize that we were not a gang. On market days we'd pester the stall-holders, offering to do little chores for them. If they didn't let us, we made a lot of noise around the stalls and this drove the customers away. Then, because most of us were hungry most of the time, we might grab something from a stall and run like the devil. 'Gan on yem ti ya Ma afore ah bat ye!' they yelled after us.

We used to beg them to give us their empty wooden crates to break up into kindling wood which we tried to sell, particularly to old ladies, who tended to be kindly disposed towards children. We didn't have a lot of success with this as there were grown-ups who made a business of it; they bought the crates off the stallholders, and pushed their bundles of kindling around on small handcarts.

We collected jam jars to take to the rag and bone merchant, and if we had amassed enough we might get a ha'penny for our troubles. Occasionally, one of these artful old dodgers would take our wares and then try to get rid of us by threatening to call the police. When that happened, woe to him! His life would be intolerable for a few days, until we got fed up and went off to pester someone else. There was one skinflint we got even with by climbing into his premises and stealing our jam jars back, not to mention taking one or two other odds and ends, and then selling them to him the next day.

* * *

I suppose I was a pretty normal seven-year-old: thoughtless, disobedient, and with a head full of dreams. But it could not escape my notice that my mother's health was failing rapidly. She never seemed to go to bed. We children slept in the bedroom; she sat up all night in her rocking chair. I know this because she'd wake me at all hours to make up the fire.

My aunt from the flat below often came up now to cook for us. I remember one morning – my father was home on one of his rare visits – she had fried some bacon for breakfast as a special treat. It was too fat for William to eat, and Da flew into a rage. He chased William all over the flat, eventually dragging him out from under the bed and thrashing him. Poor Ma, too weak to intervene, could only look on helplessly, and my aunt dared not lift a finger to come to William's aid.

To give Ma some respite during the school holidays, I was sent to stay with my maternal grandparents, who lived in the little mining village of New Washington, some six miles away. I really looked forward to these visits, although New Washington was nothing like as interesting a place as my home town. Uncle Billie used to come and collect me. Apart from Ma, he was the only member of my mother's family for whom I had any real affection or respect. There was no close feeling between my father and his parents-in-law, so it's surprising he sanctioned these visits. Perhaps he did it for Ma's sake, knowing how sick she was.

For what turned out to be my last such visit, Uncle Billie arrived to collect me on a borrowed bicycle, as his own was being repaired. This was a racing model with dropped handlebars and there was little room on the crossbar. Nevertheless, a cushion was strapped to it, I was lifted aboard and we set off. We had not got beyond the South Shields town boundary before the cushion slipped, my foot caught in the front wheel and we were both thrown off. I broke my ankle and one of the spokes pierced right through my leg; I bear the scar to this day.

I was carried into a nearby butcher's shop to await an ambulance; my holiday in New Washington was ending before it had begun, in the Ingham Infirmary. How long I was kept there I cannot recall, nor can I imagine how the bill was paid, or by whom, and history does not relate what happened to Uncle Billie and the borrowed bicycle. When I finally left the infirmary I couldn't walk, I had to be pushed everywhere in an old-fashioned folding wooden wheelchair, but I did manage to have a few days with my grandparents before returning home.

I still had to visit the outpatients' clinic and it fell to Ma to push me the two miles there and back; I simply don't know how she managed it. Furthermore, I was no longer able to help with the younger children or the household chores and, as far as I recall, she received no support from any of her family. They knew, of course, how ill she was, they also knew my father was in the sanatorium, but they did not do a thing. The only member of the Telford family who ever visited us was Uncle Billie.

I feel that my accident marked the beginning of the end of my education. My ankle took a long while to heal and all this time I was off school. I may have been a mischievous brat, but I loved lessons and was quite bright. I was good at spelling and dictation, not quite so good at arithmetic, but I managed to hold my own.

It can only have been a matter of months after my ankle had healed that my dear mother died, at the age of twenty-seven from the dreaded consumption. It was the day after my eighth birthday. Memory plays strange tricks, and I am surprised that my recollection of this momentous and tragic event is so fragmentary. I hadn't remembered, for example, that Ma didn't die at home; it was not until I looked again at her death certificate that I took in the fact that she died at 1 Moor Lane, West Harton, the sanatorium where Da was being treated. When was she moved there? I assume it was when she was very close to the end. Who looked after us when she was taken away, how the news was broken to us, and by whom, I do not recall. I believe they brought her body home immediately after she died, for I have this memory of being ushered quickly out of the house, and when I returned, I don't know how many hours later, the paper blinds had been lowered half way down the windows.

On the day of the funeral, the coffin was still open in the bedroom, resting across two trestles. Just before the lid was screwed down, I was led in and someone, I can't say who, lifted me up and held me over it. I wish profoundly that this had not been done.

Six months earlier, Eva's tiny coffin had been carried by my father's brothers; my mother's was borne on a hearse drawn by a single black horse. Was it, I wondered, one of those I had so often watched being groomed? This much I remember; also, the white handkerchief with a black border that I was given, for never in my life had I owned a handkerchief. Of the funeral service, the return to our house for refreshments, I remember nothing; I cannot even say, apart from my father, who was there.

I felt utterly bereft. Nothing could have prepared me for the terrible emptiness that I experienced. My mother's death affected me so deeply that I have, ever since, tried to impress

Fig 10. *I felt utterly bereft. Nothing could have prepared me for the terrible emptiness that I experienced. My mother's death affected me so deeply that I have, ever since, tried to impress upon all the young people I came into contact with that they should cherish their mothers.*

upon all the young people I came into contact with that they should cherish their mothers.

*   *   *

I have already said that Ganny Moffett lived just a stone's throw from Heugh Street, and she was somebody I preferred to keep out of the way of. My grandfather had died in the Great War, and since then she'd lived alone in one room in a cul-de-sac called Ladies Walk. We now moved in with her: my sister, two brothers, myself, and my father – when he was home from the sanatorium.

Most of the furniture we had while Ma was still with us had to go. All we retained was the wardrobe-type bed for my brothers and me; a pair of beautiful brass candlesticks, which I understand were a wedding present; a framed photograph of my father in his uniform, flanked by the union jack and the crest of the Durham Light Infantry; and one of those silk flags I mentioned supplied by a cigarette company.

Our new quarters measured approximately nineteen feet by nineteen, and were grossly over-furnished. The one room contained a double bed, in which Da and Mary slept, the wardrobe-type bed, Ganny's rocking chair pushed into a corner, and her peculiar slatted wooden chair-bed. In addition, there was a table, some wooden chairs, and a fine Welsh dresser, which took up half of one wall from the door to the only window, and on which was displayed a never-used set of willow-pattern china. Ganny's one luxury item was a big square wind-up gramophone on which she used to play 'Tip toe through the tulips' and 'Roses round the door'. The one other record I remember there being was 'Climb up on my knee sonny-boy', and this belonged to Da.

Fig 11. *My grandfather had died in the Great War and since then Ganny Moffett lived alone in one room in a cul-de-sac called Ladies Walk.*

A bucket containing water for drinking and cooking was kept on the bottom shelf of the dresser; it had to be filled every day from the communal tap in the yard. Also outside in the yard was the communal midden, a wide wooden plank with a hole cut in the centre balanced across a container of quick lime, which was emptied from time to time by the night-soil men. Each household supplied itself with small squares of cut-up newspaper – all very primitive. We had to go down to the communal wash house to perform our ablutions, and in winter the cold ensured that these were rudimentary. Friday night was the exception. Once a week a large oval galvanised tub was filled with water, and we took it in turns to sit in it and bath in front of the fire. Da, I remember, used to go the public baths, and it cost him one penny – and in those days there were 240 pence to the pound.

Ganny lived on the upper floor of a tenement block which housed four other families. In a two-room flat across the landing lived my father's other sister, Aunt Maggie, with her husband, Uncle Alex, and their four children: Arthur, Albert, Una and Peggy. There was also another gentleman, a retired seaman, always referred to as uncle, but I think he was no relation. I imagine he was there to help out with the family budget.

Compared with us, these members of the family appeared very affluent. They seemed to spend their weekends playing cards, dominoes, or housey-housey; and they obviously played for money, as there were always little piles of it on the table. My cousins were more or less the same age as us, and I admit to feeling somewhat jealous of them.

Despite being on the upper floor, we had no view from our single window as, once again, we looked out on a long high wall, this time of the Northern Bus Company's garage. Ladies Walk, as I have said, was a cul-de-sac and it provided us with a large rectangular area in which we could play quite safely. We must have kicked up quite a din, as we were often shouted at for making too much noise, though not when Ganny was around. She would have her rocking chair brought down, and would sit there rocking and watching us play. She must have realised we needed to burn up our childish energy as, far from putting a damper on our games, she took our side against those who wanted to shut us up.

The neighbourhood was teeming with life. Right at the top of Ladies Walk, near the main road, was the People's Mission, where I went to Sunday School. I still have the song book I was given as a prize; the date of the presentation is 1932. At the back of our tenement was Warne's ice-cream factory, and in a building nextdoor the owner kept his horses and ice-cream carts. Also nearby was a shop selling tripe and home-made black puddings. Lawson's brickyard had once occupied the bottom of the cul-de-sac, but all that remained was a large pit that had filled up with water and sludge. A boy had drowned here, consequently the place was out of bounds to us, and the council was trying to fill it in with refuse brought in horse-drawn carts. I couldn't resist hanging around this insalubrious spot, because on one side of the pit there were a number of pigeon lofts.

* * *

Before Ma died I'd had little to do with Ganny Moffett. She'd always seemed a stern figure, and I was uncomfortable in her presence. For this reason I never dropped in on her; in fact, I deliberately kept out of her way. I did make the odd visit in the company of my father, but I never remember her coming to our place, even after Ma became so ill.

I can see her now, short and stout, with her rather lank grey hair twisted into a bun. Her long black skirts reached down to her ankles, and she wore an apron made of sacking and a shawl. On her head there perched an old peaked cap, which she took off only in bed.

After we moved in with Ganny, I got the impression we were in the way all the time; also, I was strongly aware that she favoured my brother George and sister Mary. The reasons for this are not hard to see: George had been named after Da's twin brother, who was killed at Mons; and, with his mop of blond curls, he was the spitting image of Ganny's boy at that age. As for Mary, she was a little dark-haired beauty, and everyone bowed to her slightest whim. I was quite soon to realise the reason for the indulgence she received.

Mary had been ailing for a long time, and stayed in bed more or less continuously after we moved in with Ganny. A lot of the day she just drifted in and out of sleep, and sometimes, when her fever rose, she'd grow delirious. I don't remember her eating, but she used to sip drinks to ease her persistent coughing and wheezing. One day Ganny, who was a stickler for tidiness, came in and found a cup Mary had used that had not been replaced on its hook. When she asked who was responsible for this lapse, Mary whispered 'Tom'. Whether this was in answer to Ganny's question, or whether it was part of some feverish hallucination, I shall never know, but I am certain that I was not the culprit; I knew better than to offend in this way. But, despite my protestations of innocence, I was roundly chastised and, naturally, felt indignant. However, my indignation soon turned to remorse as, shortly after this incident, Mary passed away. Less than three months after Ma's death, she was carried off by acute pulmonary tuberculosis, compounded by whooping cough. Our family of seven had now been reduced to four.

The only thing that sticks in my mind about Mary's funeral is the 'feast' that was held afterwards. Why, oh why, were all these grown-up people eating and drinking – not just tea, but beer and spirits – when I had just lost my only remaining sister? These were nearly all relations, and they seemed to be enjoying themselves; it made no sense to me.

* * *

Living in someone else's house is very different from living in your own home. When Ma was alive, of course I was told off and punished for my misdemeanours; but I didn't have to ask permission to move about, to be on my best behaviour, to mind my Ps and Qs. Anyone who has lived in lodgings will know what I mean; and this feeling of never being really and truly at home persisted until I married and finally had a place of my own.

'Gan on hadaway doon ti the sands, afor as york your hide for ye!' Ganny always seemed to be saying; and this is most probably why I spent so much time outside. She kept a tawse hanging on the end of the mantelpiece, and when I saw her eyeing this, I'd dodge nimbly out of her way, but she'd wag her finger and say, 'Ye'll be coming yem, and ah'll get a had o' ye then.'

I had one very good pal called Joe, who lived a couple of doors away from us. I used to call for him in the morning, and we'd take the short walk to school together. I don't know why we got on so well, as Joe was a much more subdued child than I was. He wore spectacles, without which he was almost blind; in fact, later in life he did go blind and earned his living teaching the piano. His mother was always very watchful of him, and there were times when he was not allowed to play with the rest of us. Children can be very cruel to one another, but I'm happy to say Joe was not teased about his affliction. Perhaps this was because he was a very nice, quiet lad, who'd grown up with all of us kids, and he came from a good family.

It was Joe's uncle who owned the tripe shop up the street, and on Tuesday evenings Joe and I used to go there to watch, and 'help' in the making of the black puddings for which he was quite famous locally – my mouth waters at the memory of them. There were vats of pigs' blood standing around, and I recall the skins being stretched over a funnel, down which the filling was stuffed, before they were twisted every six inches to make strings of puddings, which were then cooked. I was allowed to stay out later on Tuesday evenings, and was always given a black pudding to take home. I looked forward to these visits, especially in the winter, as the shop was a very warm place, with fires burning under the coppers where the puddings were boiled, and full of delicious smelling steam.

My cousin Arthur and Joe's elder brother were the two leaders of the pack of Ladies Walk kids. They decided what was what, and had the last word when decisions were made. We spent quite a bit of time hanging around the stables at the ice-cream factory, helping the men hitch the horses to the carts and hoping for a ride down to the place where they were loaded. We were never allowed on the carts once they were loaded, and the only ice cream we ever had was what we managed to pinch. Who knows, it might not have tasted so good had we been given it. If there were too many of us the men would send us packing; but in the evenings, when no one was about, we'd return to the stables and climb up into the hay loft, where we romped about.

We also spent a lot of time in the boarded-in space beneath my Uncle Foster's pigeon loft, which was in the tenement yard. We made candles out of the tallow from the tripe shop, and on dark nights would huddle over their guttering flames telling stories and jokes. I don't know how much success my uncle had with his pigeons; now and again he'd breed one that was good enough to race, and it would be packed into a wicker basket and taken to the station, to be transported to some distant place from which it would be released.

*   *   *

I didn't see a great deal of my father at this time, although I know he signed himself out of the sanatorium after Mary died. What drove him to do this, I cannot say – it could have been dejection or just bloody-mindedness. He was certainly not cured. I assumed he was spending most of his time at the Scotia Bar or the Turk's Head. I don't think he was employed, so where the money came from I know not, unless he had a war pension.

Ganny was now taking all the decisions about the welfare of me and my brothers; Da was either too dejected or too ill to concern himself with his three remaining children. This once volatile and unpredictable man had become completely listless. Obviously, he was deeply affected by losing his wife and two daughters all within the space of less than a year, but I was too young to understand what was going on. I realise now that he must have been in deep mourning, his grief about the loss of my mother compounded, perhaps, by remorse.

On one memorable occasion, however, Da did exercise parental control. There was a family living in the next tenement block to ours whom he forbade us to have anything to do with. I liked the mother; she was a nice person, but she had to manage on her own, as most of the time her husband was at sea, and she had no control over her two boys. The elder, a lad some eighteen months older than myself, was a real tearaway. He had been taken to court a couple of times for stealing, and it was said locally that he was just one step away from reform school. As a general rule he didn't associate with the rest of us kids from Ladies Walk; he spent most of his time in another part of town with a hard gang that managed to keep one jump ahead of the law.

One afternoon, when William, George, and I were hanging around the market place, we ran into the two brothers, and, forgetting Da's injunctions, tagged along with them. The elder one produced a sum of money and a bunch of keys – I gave not a thought to where these might have come from – and decided we'd all go to the cinema. Off we trouped, though I knew that my brothers and I had strict instructions to be home at 3.30 in order to be washed and got ready for a British Legion children's Christmas tea party and concert, for which Da had obtained tickets. None of us could tell the time, and I recall asking an old gentleman who was sitting in the back row what time it was. 'There's a bloody clock up there!' he growled, so I suspect I had disturbed his nap, and I was too frightened to tell him I couldn't read it. I returned to my seat till the end of the film.

It was 5 o'clock by the time we got home, too late for the

bun fight. Da was livid. He asked George where we'd been, and he came out with the whole story, including whom we'd been with. That, of course, was the last straw. I, being the eldest, was made the example and got the thrashing. We were washed and put to bed, and Da stormed out.

When he had been gone a safe length of time, Ganny got us up and dressed, and sent us off to the concert with a note excusing us for not attending the tea party. She did not need to impress upon us that we were to come straight home as soon as it was over, in order to be safely back in bed before Da returned; I was not going to risk a second thrashing, with Da's fury fuelled by drink.

The cinema provided pure escapism and a running topic of conversation for us kids. I was film mad, which is probably why I allowed myself to be led so imprudently into the previous misadventure. Occasionally I was given a ha'penny for running a message for someone, and if I was lucky enough to receive two such rewards in one week it would be the crock of gold at the end of the rainbow, for it enabled me to go to the 'penny rush' at the picture house. You sat on the edge of your seat in the dark, eyes glued to the silver screen, while Tom Mix, the cowboy hero, picked off the baddies, or Tarzan came swinging through the jungle, or Pearl White lay tied to the railway line as the express train bore down upon her. These were silent films and I couldn't read all the subtitles, but who needed subtitles? We had the pianist, who provided the perfect soundtrack, revving up our excitement with music that galloped and thundered to match the action unreeling before us. Each episode broke off at its most dramatic point, and the message would flash up on the screen: 'Will Tom Mix get his man? Do not miss next week's episode.' 'Will Pearl White escape? Come next week and see for yourself.' It was important to hang on to your ticket, as sometimes, halfway through the programme, numbers would be flashed up on the screen, and if they matched those on your ticket you would receive a bar of toffee, or an orange, sometimes even a free ticket for next week's showing. Alas, my lucky number never came up.

One cinema used to run a children's mid-week matinée at 4.15, after school had finished. You went in at one of the side doors, and threw your penny on to a table at which a gentleman was sitting. Other kids seemed to come by the necessary penny more easily than I did. I often had to resort to ingenuity and deviousness to get the wherewithal for the 'penny rush', never mind the mid-week show. On one occasion – whether out of bravado, or just from a longing to go in with my friends, I don't recall – I tried to sidle in behind two of them as they were paying, but the man on the door spotted what I was up to. 'Hey, you young bugger, where's your penny?' I said I'd thrown it on to the table like the others, but he grabbed me. 'No, you didn't, you lying little bugger.' And he boxed me around the ears and, literally, kicked me out. 'Gan on and bugger off!' I cried all the way home. Of course I'd brought this on my own head so there was no one I could turn to for comfort, but at least the story never got to Da's ears.

* * *

I have already said I used to spend a lot of time on the beach, and in the summer months this increased. Ganny's parting words were always, 'Divant gan near the wata!' But there was little danger we would disobey on summer Sunday afternoons, as we liked to go to the beach fair. In those days Sunday was the Lord's day and the fair was not open, so we'd find a gap in the boards at the rear and squeeze through. Once inside, we made straight for the slide; as there were no mats on hand we went down on our bottoms, picking ourselves up straight away and dashing back up the steps for another go. The more excited we got the more noise we made, so inevitably we'd get caught and sent packing. I'm happy to say, however, we were only having fun, and it would never have occurred to any of us to vandalise the place.

One Sunday, William, George, and I ran into our maternal grandfather and step-grandmother, who were on an outing to the beach with their young family. They bought us all ice creams and then took us to the beach studio to be photographed. That night I told Ganny what had happened, and she told Da. He was furious, and dashed off a letter to his father-in-law, telling him in no uncertain terms that if he wished to have us photographed he should, in future, obtain his permission.

There had long been bad feeling between the two men. My mother's father had been against the marriage; and Da, on numerous occasions, had been deceived by his father-in-law. The story of the gold watch still rankles, but I did not hear it until I was grown up. It seems that on my parents' wedding day there was a great deal of drinking, and by early evening the supply of spirits had run out. My grandfather was sent down to the pub for a bottle of whisky, but, as he had no ready cash, he was to hand over my father's gold watch as collateral, and Da, who was a friend of the landlord, would redeem it the following day. Half an hour later, he returned without the whisky and without the watch. His story was that he had dropped the bottle in the road on the way home, but when Da went to settle up with the landlord the next day he learned that no transaction had taken place.

Years later, I was shown a gold watch in my grandfather's possession, but I was never allowed to hold it and open it, and I am convinced this is because it had the name William Gray Moffett inscribed in it. After my grandfather's death, I wrote to the family about this watch, but the reply I received was evasive: there may have been a gold watch, but it had probably been sold to pay for the medicines grandfather had needed just before he died. This excuse does not stand up, since my grandfather died at a time when medicines were free on the NHS.

*   *   *

When I think of the other members of my family, on both sides, I realise how sagacious Ganny Moffett was. To me, she was an old lady, but in the early 1930s – I don't know the exact year of her birth – she would only have been in her late fifties or early sixties, which is no great age by today's standards. Of course, nothing ages a person more than poverty, and Ganny's life had been both hard and sad. She had lost her husband and two sons in the Great War, and stood no chance of remarrying, as a whole generation of young men had been wiped out. When you saw her, the first things you noticed were the lines etched deep into her face, the hard set of her mouth, and her sallow complexion. However, beneath the forbidding exterior, there was a compassionate heart, as I was always discovering when I least expected it.

I used to suffer intermittently from boils, and Ganny would tear up rags and encase my knees in bread poultices. These were so hot that I used to cry when she applied them. I dreaded the treatment, but have to admit it worked. One day, during a siege of boils, I was out playing tag in Ladies Walk; I tore round the corner and ran slap into a curmudgeonly old man who lived across the street. He lashed out with his stick and I yelped with pain as he caught me across the knees. Blood spurted out and poured down my legs. 'Serves yer reet, yer bloody young hooligan. If ah had ma way I'd gi' ye mare than that. I'd bat yer lugs.' As luck would have it, Ganny happened to be standing at the gate to our back yard and saw everything for herself, because if I'd gone home with bleeding knees and explained what had happened, and Ganny had gone to tackle our surly neighbour, it would have been his word against mine, and grown-ups tend to believe grown-ups. But she had witnessed the incident and was off after the old man. She gave him 'the length of her tongue', as she would have put it, and, if she could, I'm sure she'd have wrested his stick from his hand and whacked him.

I had my regular chores to do, and Ganny was an exacting taskmistress. It was my job to fill the pail of drinking water every day from the tap in the yard; to take the sack down to the coal merchant's in the next street and hump two stone of coal – for which Ganny paid tuppence – up the stairs on my back. I was also expected to clean the washhouse, which was used by the five families in the tenement. This, as I have said, is where we washed ourselves, except on bath nights, and it was the place where all the laundry was done. It contained a large copper, heated by a coal fire, in which clothes and sheets were possed – pounded by a long wooden pole before being squeezed through the wooden rollers of the heavy mangle. The handle of the mangle was held down by a split pin, and, when I was monkeying about with this instead of getting on with the cleaning, it flew out and the handle jerked up splitting my upper lip. Once again, I had to be taken to hospital and stitched up. Ganny was really cross, but at the same time, I think, worried enough to refrain from giving me a backhander.

Every evening I had to take Ganny's beautiful hand-painted tulip jug to the Wellington to have it filled with beer. I didn't need to go into the bar – in fact, I shouldn't have been allowed in – as round at the side was the bottle-and-jug entrance. The price of this nightly tipple was one penny.

Ganny never touched a drop until we children were tucked up in bed, but after a while, when the drink began to take effect, I, in my corner of the room, would hear her talking to herself – or was this her way of telling me things? She lay back in her reclining chair, with the firelight flickering on her lined face, and rambled on about the past. It seems that there was a time when the family had considerably more money. My grandfather, whom I never knew, was a stone mason, and had helped make and install the stone lifeboat that still stands on top of the South Shields town hall; he never came back from the trenches. She talked about Da being gassed and shot in the head during the Great War, and about his twin brother George, killed at Mons, and another son, just turned sixteen, who was killed on the Somme. She would say she could see pictures of dear Ma reflected in the flames, and that Ma had been a very sick girl before she died. These were the only occasions she ever mentioned my mother; the rest of the time she might never have existed.

Ganny's other little indulgence was snuff, and her nostrils were stained yellow from this lifelong habit. I used to fetch the snuff from the corner shop, and it cost tuppence an ounce. 'Golden Pheasant' was her brand, and woe betide me if I came back with the wrong one.

Ganny was also a bit of a moralist, with a maxim for every occasion. She'd come out with these pretty often, so, not surprisingly, many of them have stuck in my mind. 'If there were no wicked women in this world, there would be no wicked men.' 'You should only believe half of what you hear, and nothing of what you read.' 'A fact is a lie and a half.' 'If you can't hear a woman walk, don't trust her.'

I can remember standing at the top of the street with Ganny one summer's morning, watching some of the local mothers and their children boarding a charabanc for a day's outing. The organiser turned to her and said: 'Gan on doon yem and put his good clase on, an we'll tak him wi' us.' A whole day out in a charabanc! I felt a surge of wild excitement, but Ganny wasn't having it. The woman tried to persuade her, I pleaded with her, but she would not budge. On our way home I complained bitterly. 'Children', said Ganny, 'should be seen and not heard.'

Her reason for not allowing me to go on the outing was her obstinate refusal to accept what she considered charity. Occasionally, when I ran a message for a neighbour, I would receive a small reward – a bun, a bit of home-made toffee, a precious ha'penny – and I'd volunteer my services again in the hope that something would come my way. Ganny frowned on this and did her best to discourage the neighbours from rewarding me. My father, as I've said, had strong feelings about begging; and once I was grown up I myself, so my wife would tell me, would never ask favours or accept charity. We Moffetts are a proud and stubborn lot.

* * *

The thrashings I could accept; I'd done wrong – though what

constituted wrong-doing was not always apparent to me –
and I paid the price. What I could never accept was the mental
hurt. Grown-up people tend to think that if they wipe a
child's tears and pat it on the head, that's the end of the
matter; but children not only have a keen sense of what is fair
and what is unfair, their feelings can be wounded too. Many's
the time I'd creep away to nurse my anguish and cry bitterly
over some hurt, and I'd eat my heart out over matters that I
know a grown-up would have considered trivial, but to me
seemed unjust.

A case in point is the favouritism Ganny showed to my
cousin Arthur, who lived with my aunt Maggie in the flat
across the landing. If he ran a message for her, she'd reward
him, sometimes even with a penny that got him into the
'penny rush'. She used to knit him socks, even though he had
a mother and a father who were not hard up, and I was running around barefoot. Perhaps she thought that if I had no
shoes, I didn't need socks. Or was it because Arthur was
Ganny's daughter's child, and she thought more of her daughter than of her son? Or were we my father, brothers and I –
a burden that she resented? Whatever the explanation, the
unfairness was hard for me to accept.

Da used to cut our hair at home, using borrowed clippers
and scissors. William and George were easy to work on, as
both had curly hair; mine was stiff and straight. After hacking
away at it and getting nowhere, he threw down the clippers
and pulled a penny out of his pocket. 'Gan on doon to the
barber's, ah canna cut this bloody barbed wire.' When I
returned, Da blew his top for the barber had close-cropped
my head leaving a fringe that flopped over my forehead. I
understand he never spoke to the barber again, but the first

flush of his fury was vented on me, and for weeks, until my hair had grown back, he called me baldy.

We were never starving, but there were times when we suffered terrible pangs of hunger. There was no question of raiding the larder, as my children were able to do; for one thing, there was no larder! Whenever I was hungry, I went off on the scrounge. I'd offer to run messages in the hope of earning a bite to eat; I'd ask the local greengrocer if he had any bruised fruit, or hang around at Wright's biscuit factory up the road hoping I might get a handful of broken biscuits. As a last resort, I went to the market place where, I have to confess, I resorted to stealing fruit and other things to eat by reaching through the tarpaulin at the back of the stalls. I became quite an expert, or else I was very lucky, for I was never caught. Once or twice I came near it. 'Aa'l gie ye a skelp i' the lug! Aa'l skin ye if I get a had o' ye!' But I'd taken to my heels. Had I ever been arrested, Ganny would have died of shame.

Normally, when I felt things were not fair I kept quiet, but I did, on one occasion, speak out. I'd been sent to bed early for some misdemeanour and was feeling hard done by. I complained that I had no shoes or socks, and only one shirt, which I was wearing in bed. For this bit of selfpity I got a tanning with the tawse and was told not to have so much lip. 'I grumbled because I had not shoes until I met a man who had not feet', quoted Ganny before proceeding to lecture me with her usual solemnity. If I looked about me, she said, I would always see someone who was worse off than I was.

This was no consolation. What did Ganny mean? Da never played with us, he never put us to bed, he was never even around at bedtime unless he'd sent us to bed for a punishment. He never mentioned Ma, yet I suppose he thought about her and missed her as much as I did. I felt, perhaps wrongly, that it must have been easier for him; he was, after all, back living with his mother, and therefore had much more freedom than I. We boys were merely lodgers in Ganny's place; he was back home.

I can imagine some of the thoughts and feelings he may have had, for when my first wife died I was left with a seven-year-old boy, the difference being that I had no mother to return to. But despite his sorrow and his outbursts of violence, I believe he did love his children, and I know that he was our Da and we loved him, no matter what.

I now realise that when Ganny was reproving me for my 'lip' she must have been feeling anxiety and despair for us children, for, unbeknown to us, Da was dying. Not long after this incident, early one evening when I was out playing, my cousin came looking for me. I was to collect up William and George and come home immediately. As we entered Ganny's place someone said, 'Dinna clash the door hinney.' And I recall someone else saying, 'He'll niver put ower the neet. He's in a sad way.'

The room was full of people gathered around my father's bed. Why were they all here? Why was Da lying in bed? What was my maternal grandfather doing; he'd never set foot in this building, but here he was, along with a crowd of my father's relatives. What was going on?

The three of us were propelled to the side of the bed to be addressed by our father, who lectured us on our behaviour and told us to be good boys. He had special words for me. 'Yer gannen wi' ya granda tiv his heyem, hinney. Diven gi' na bother. Put te reets the two bairns, there's a canny lad. Ye a gan a be the fether noo.'

It all seemed so solemn, yet I imagined we were going to grandfather Telford's house in New Washington for a holiday. Ganny packed our few clothes; we were then quickly ushered out of the room, and went with our grandfather to catch the bus that would take us to his home. It was dark when we arrived at our destination, and we were sent straight to bed. When we came down the next day, our grandfather told us that Da had died at 6 o'clock that morning; at the age of thirty-seven he had fallen victim to Phthisis Pulmonalis (or TB). It was 9th November 1933; I was ten-and-a-half years old.

It suddenly dawned on me why we had been brought here, why it had all happened so quickly, and why Da had told me to look after William and George. My world had been torn apart. Would there be no end to the destruction of my family? I went out of the back door, through the small yard and into the street crying my heart out. How long I stayed out there I do not know; eventually my grandfather's youngest daughter, Lillian, came after me. She tried to console me and get me to come back indoors. I should have been looking after my two young brothers, but my grief drove all thoughts of them from my mind.

When tragedy strikes everyone seems willing to help, and nothing is too much trouble. But it soon becomes a chore, and altruism and benevolence go out of the window. It did not take long for me to learn what all those relatives had been discussing round my father's deathbed; they had been arguing with him about the future of his sons. They wanted to split us up: William should go to Uncle Foster and his wife, George should stop with Ganny Moffett, where he would also be under the wing of Aunt Maggie across the landing, and I should go to New Washington. But Da, in his wisdom, had resisted their pressure and insisted we stay together. Despite his dislike and distrust of his father-in-law, he realised he was the only relative capable of taking the three of us.

Three days later we returned to South Shields for the funeral; Da was to be buried alongside dear Ma and my sisters Eva and Mary. There were a lot of people there, many of them relatives, for the Moffett clan is a large one. There was also a contingent of Da's buddies. It was the day after Armistice Day, and as these men filed past the open grave each dropped his poppy on to the coffin. After the customary eating and drinking, all I can remember is that we were whisked away once more.

* * *

Our new home was very different from any place we had lived in. Of course I'd stayed there on several occasions and had a lovely time, but that's not the same as moving in. We had come from Ganny's cluttered single room, in which at one time six of us were living; we now found ourselves in a whole house. It had a front room, a living room, three bedrooms upstairs, plus a small box-bedroom halfway up the stairs, a kitchen-cum-bathroom, a scullery, and, in the high-walled back yard, a flushing WC – something unknown in any of the houses we'd lived in – adjacent to which stood a spacious well-stocked coal shed.

As was the custom in those days, the front room was used only on special occasions; the curtains were kept closed most of the time, and it was out of bounds to us. On the mantel-piece there stood a beautiful Hornby electric train, in green LNER livery, that belonged to my grandfather's youngest child, John. He never played with it, and no one was allowed to touch it; in fact, it was seldom even seen, as the front room was used so little. The most used room in the house was, as you would expect, the living room, which contained a large fireplace with a cooking range. The fire box was the centre-piece with, on the right hand, a copper for heating water, which was carried into the kitchen in a bucket, and on the left an oven. All of the bread eaten in this household was made by my stepgrandmother, or her daughters, who both did their share of the cooking.

Opposite the cooking range a wooden plaque with poker-work lettering hung on the wall.

> It's easy enough to be pleasant
>> When life flows along like a song,
> But the man worthwhile
> Is the man who can smile
>> When everything goes dead wrong.

There was also a wireless fixed to the wall, out of the reach of children. No one was allowed to touch it except grand-father, and he used it just once a day, to listen to the six o'clock news. Everyone had to keep completely silent during the fifteen-minute bulletin; indeed, if the weather permitted, we boys were sent outside while the news was on. Before we came to live with my grandparents I'd never heard the wire-less in a house.

The front bedroom was occupied by my grandparents, and we boys were never allowed into it. My grandfather's two daughters shared a smaller room, and the biggest bedroom, which contained a double and a single bed, was occupied by John and me and my two brothers. The four of us slept two-

and-two head-to-toe in the double bed. This room served also as a playroom, when the weather was too inclement for us to be outside, and contained a quarter-size billiard table, a beautiful old rocking horse and a number of other toys. As I recollect, I was allowed to play with the toys in this room, but William and George were not; they were always being pushed outside just to get them out of the way. Apart from the bulbous-ended torch Da gave me one Christmas, and my gord, I'd never had any toys. The first Christmas I spent at my grandfather's I was given a splendid toy crane; it was solidly made of metal, brightly painted, and it worked – my pride and joy. I was not to enjoy it for long.

All the objects in the house, not to mention the spaciousness of the house itself, made my grandfather appear as a man of means. His house was another world to us. It was, however, a world in which we were not welcome. Our other homes may have been cramped and squalid, but they had a human warmth which was now completely lacking. Obviously the most important thing in our lives had been our mother's love for us, but when that was taken away we still had a father; and Ganny, for all her forbidding exterior, did love us. There was also the companionship of the other Ladies Walk kids, and the network of aunts and uncles and cousins who lived all around. Times were hard, but there was a kind of solidarity and warmth that had enabled us children to feel carefree.

My maternal grandfather, as I have said, had two families. I know nothing of his first wife; his children by her had been Ma, her sisters Maggie and Sarah, and my Uncle Billie. They were all, of course, of a different generation from me, and by the time we arrived to live in New Washington they had left home. Alas, my beloved Uncle Billie had been told to pack his

Fig 12. My mother's family
Back row left to right: Isa, Uncle Billie, Sarah
Middle row left to right: Maggie, Lillian, Granddad, Grandma, Rhoda, Ma; *Front row:* John

bags and get out, and he had gone South and found work as a projectionist at the Victoria Cinema in Cambridge.

My grandfather married for the second time a woman who was quite a lot younger than him; I suppose she must have been in her mid-forties at the time we came to live with them, but she looked older than her years: tall, haggard, and clad in long black skirts – a witch (without a broom stick). When she took me shopping with her, to carry her bags, she'd go all dressed up with a big wide-brimmed hat. She was no blood relation of mine, and there was no love lost between us either. In the past, when I'd gone to stay in New Washington, she'd been nice enough to me, and I'd been allowed to do more or less as I liked; after we moved in permanently, I realised this was no holiday.

Her manner was very peremptory, and she had none of Ganny Moffett's sagacity. There was no question our using the familiar 'ganny' with her – not that we would have wanted to – she said we were to address her as grandma. She showed us no warmth or compassion; indeed she made it very clear that we were there on sufferance . I think she must have had a lot of anger bottled up inside her, which she would take out on my brothers. She was always thrashing them, and William, who had a somewhat truculent character, would retaliate, which of course only made matters worse.

She had three daughters. The eldest, Isabel, or Isa as she was always known, was about twenty-two. We saw very little of her; she went out to work and, shortly after we arrived, she married. Rhoda, the next daughter, was about six years older than me, which would make her sixteen or seventeen at that time, and she was the best of the bunch, an unassuming girl, who seemed to have no wish to lord it over us. She wouldn't stand any nonsense, but you knew where you were with her and she was good fun, for she was quite a tomboy and had a very dry sense of humour. Rhoda didn't go out to work, though in the season she went potato picking at the local farm. She stayed at home and did the housework and most of the cooking.

Lillian was just nine months older than me, and she could be a silly, vain, opinionated creature. When she was in a good mood, I could get anything out of her, but she'd get on her high horse and insist we all call her auntie, especially when we were outside, as she fancied her dignity was increased by this title. I was the one she knew best, and there were times when she treated me almost like a brother; she hardly knew William and George till they moved in, and she behaved atrociously towards them.

The youngest child, John, was three months younger than George. He was a spoilt mother's boy, a sneak and a telltale.

Granddad escaped the hardship that affected so many in the 1930s. He was employed by the local corporation as a foreman in the roads and highways department; this was a good job and he was highly respected. He used to take his bait and a can of tea with him when he left for work each morning, unless he was working near home, in which case he would have a hot lunch delivered to him on site. One of us youngsters – generally me – would have to hurry home from school to carry out this task. He might have a meat pie, or pudding, and vegetables, sandwiched between two plates which were wrapped in a large red and white spotted handkerchief tied at the corners, and a fresh can of hot tea. No dawdling on the way, or the meal would be cold on arrival. He seemed to take great pride in showing me off to the men who worked under him, introducing his eldest grandchild, and telling them that he was bringing up me and my two brothers since our parents had passed on. This made the men behave kindly towards me; they'd invite me to come and sit beside them, offer me a sandwich from their bait. It was quite a privilege taking Granddad his lunch, and I loved doing it, even if it meant dashing back to be in time for afternoon school.

Granddad was the head of the household, and when he was at home he didn't have to lift a finger; he was treated like a king. Strangely enough, though, it was Grandma who had the last word. If, for example, someone wanted permission to do something, he'd ask, 'What did Mother say?' 'Mother said "No".' 'Well, that's it, isn't it?'

One other person lived in the house, a lodger named Ralph. He was corporation workman, one of Granddad's men, and he occupied the little box-bedroom. He appeared only for meals, which he took with the family, and then he'd go up to his room. He was pleasant enough to us boys, giving us a nod or the time of day when he met us, but he was extremely retiring. I don't think I've ever known a quieter man than Ralph.

There's no doubt that our living conditions and our diet were much better than anything we'd known previously. We began wearing shoes regularly for the first time in our lives, paid for, perhaps, out of the seven shillings and sixpence weekly orphans' pension our grandparents now received. The house was warm and dry, and there was always a plentiful supply of plain food on the table. My brothers and I were not offered the same food as the immediate family and the lodger, but we never went hungry. At mealtimes we had to stop outside or, if the weather was rough, wait up in the big bedroom-playroom until the others had finished their meal; only then were we given ours.

On weekdays, the main meal was always taken in the evening, after Granddad came home from work. Quite often we'd have suet pudding; on one day it would be the first course served with gravy, followed by the main course; the next day the suet pudding would be served with syrup as the sweet. Living near the coast we ate a lot of fish, which was abundant and cheap: cod, herrings, and winkles for Sunday tea; it was delivered to the door by a fishmonger with a van. On Saturdays and Sundays the main meal would be served at mid-day. Sunday tea was quite a treat, for, in addition to the winkles, which you fished out of the shell with a pin, there would be bread and butter – margarine for us boys – jam, golden syrup and a selection of scones, cakes and buns. Then everyone in the household, except Granddad, would troop off to the Salvation Army service.

William, George and I spent most of our time out of the house, returning only for meals. It was better that way as we were not under surveillance, unless John was with us; he'd go back and report on us to Grandma, for he was a sneak. We got to know the neighbouring families, and I became very close to one couple named Thompson, who had no children of their own. I don't remember the lady's name, but the man's was Bob, and I used to call them uncle and aunt. I'd often have tea with them, but had to keep quiet about it, as my grandparents and the rest of their family resented it when other people favoured us in any way; whereas they themselves only made a show of tolerating us, in order to keep up appearances with the neighbours.

I was eventually forbidden to visit the Thompsons. However, I contrived to go on seeing 'Uncle Bob', for he was a gravedigger, and I used to go to the cemetery where he worked, and spent many happy hours in his company. Needless to say, Granddad found out about these visits and I was in trouble. So too was 'Uncle Bob', for Granddad went round to reproach him and forbid him to see me.

Once I was out of the house I could forget whatever was going on at home and feel reasonably carefree. We played a great deal around the back of our housing estate, where the Corporation had a storeyard. There we would climb all over their old carts and wagons. At the top of the street there was a large park, where we played all the usual ball games.

We also used to play on the slag heap of one of the local mines. Despite the fact that the family coal shed was always well stocked, Grandma would sometimes send us to rake the heap for bits of coal, a tedious and filthy job, but it was surprising how much you could collect. Every family had a barrow, known as a bogie, often a somewhat primitive vehicle, consisting perhaps of a tea chest with shafts mounted on a set of pram wheels, and you'd find all sorts of people, even old ladies, filling their bogie down at the slag heap.

As I've already said, I tended to go off on my own quite a lot. I'd often walk to Sunderland, about six miles away, to get a glimpse of my favourite football team. The gates would be reopened about ten minutes before the end of the game, so that fans who wanted to could get out before the last-minute rush, and the custodians would allow us boys in to see the last few minutes of play.

On one occasion, as I was making my way home after a match, a gentleman on a motorcycle stopped and offered me a lift. I thanked him and accepted, and he dropped me off at the corner of the street almost opposite my grandparents' front door. Unfortunately, Granddad saw me alight from the motor-cycle; I got a terrific dressing down and was told never to accept lifts from strangers again. I couldn't understand why he was so angry, or what he was objecting to. Of course I under-stand now that he was afraid I would get molested; but that sort of thing was much less prevalent than it is today.

Granddad never beat me; there was no doubt that I was his favourite, and I have to admit that I revelled in this situation, for it allowed me to have much more leeway than the others. I don't know why this should have been. Was it something to do with his feelings for Ma, or his disappointment in his own son John? He was always beating William and George, and I should have heeded Da's dying words to me and stuck up for them more. I neglected my duty towards them, and I'm not proud of myself.

After the move to New Washington I started attending Usworth School. It was a good school and I enjoyed it very much, but I had a struggle to keep up. There'd been the long period off school while my ankle was healing, and all the other upheavals in my young life undoubtedly took their toll. I found the work much more difficult, but I made a serious effort to make up for lost time. It is one of my great regrets that my education suffered in this way. I remember one of my teachers talking about me to my father on the day of Ma's funeral. 'He's a good clever lad,' she said, 'but he will chatter too much in class.'

Friday was market-day, and I used to go down to the market after school; I loved watching the stall holders selling and auctioning their goods. I got to know a fellow who had a crock and china stall, and after a while, he let me help him. I did some fetching and carrying, and wrapped up his customers' purchases. I obviously did well, as he soon invited me to come on Saturdays too, and I gradually became his right-hand man. I helped him unpack his goods and lay them out, and then I was allowed to serve and sell. Eventually, he'd leave me to look after the stall while he took a short break. Then when he'd finished for the day I'd help him repack his goods and load up his cart, and it would be goodbye till the next Friday, when I would be eagerly awaiting his return. I used to earn sixpence, which was a fortune to me, and I was being paid for something I enjoyed doing. I'd gladly have worked for nothing, as I had when I started; just being appreciated by someone was enough for me.

On Sundays we were made to attend the Salvation Army services three times a day. We sang hymns, and there were long prayer meetings, which we used to refer to as 'creeping meetings'. The sermons seemed to go on for hours, and we had to sit still and keep quiet, because even if Grandma was not there to keep an eye on us herself, some busybody would report to her on how we'd behaved, or misbehaved.

It was all a terrible bore until a new officer arrived, an industrious little woman, who seemed to love children. She was always finding new things for us to do and ways to keep us interested and occupied. She started a band, which was great fun. She put me on to the tenor horn, and taught me to play and to read music. It was very interesting and a great challenge, and I became quite adept; I could follow the music and play one or two hymn tunes. The first hymn I learnt to play was 'Fight the good fight', a nice easy one. I wish I could have kept it up; but alas, it was not to be.

I've said that Lillian was a silly, stuck-up child, unpredictable in her moods; and I was to make a stupid mistake with her. When I was foraging through the glove drawer of the hall stand, which was full of rubbish and odds and ends, I came across a sixpenny piece. I put it back where I'd found it, but told Lillian about it. Some time later I took it and went out and spent one penny of it, and hid the change, burying it in the ground alongside an old shed up the road. Lillian had the same idea, but I'd beaten her to it, so she told on me to Granddad. I wouldn't admit to taking it, and Granddad got very angry; he sat me and my brothers on the sofa and threatened us with all sorts of punishment, including calling in the policeman who lived a few doors up the street.

In the end, to save the other two, I owned up, but said 'findy-keepy'. 'A'ave a good mind to clout ya rags', said Granddad, and asked me what I'd done with it. 'Bowt a bag o' bullets' – aniseed balls, in fact, and you could get an awful lot for a penny in those days. He asked what I had done with the rest of the money, and I informed him I'd hidden it 'ower by'. He told me to fetch it, and sent Lillian with me, which was most humiliating. That, I suppose, was part of my punishment, and it served me right. Granddad took the five pence and confiscated the sweets.

I also got into trouble for borrowing John's bicycle. I used to ride off for a little fun, and it was on this machine that I'd visit 'Uncle Bob' at the cemetery. John was too scared to ride it himself, but he'd complain to his mother if I took it. Granddad didn't seem to bother much because he had taught me to ride it, and knew I was the only one who would venture out on it. But Grandma made a fuss about me taking it, and William and George were forbidden even to touch it.

About this time my feelings changed towards my grandfather, and I developed an aversion to him that was almost as strong as the one I had to his wife. He'd taken to humiliating me. 'Take the peas out of your mouth when you speak', he'd say. I didn't know what he was on about at first, then it dawned on me that I had a speech impediment, and he was mocking me; I was good for a laugh. I've never forgiven him for this; he made me self-conscious for the rest of my life, so much so that when I became a college butler I refused ever to make announcements.

* * *

We had already spent nearly a year in New Washington and in all this time had never once returned to visit Ganny in South Shields, a mere six-and-a-half miles away. She'd have had no idea how we were, and certainly had no inkling of what was in store for us.

Our moments of happiness occurred out of the house, and it was becoming increasingly obvious that my brothers and I had outstayed our welcome in the Telford household. The preparations for our departure must have been made over some months. In fact I am convinced that secret negotiations were begun shortly after my father died, and I am not prepared to forgive and forget.

The first notion we had that change might be in the air was when we were taken to the doctor to be vaccinated, without, of course, being told why. Then we were kitted out with all sorts of new clothes: pyjamas, underpants, vests – things we'd never had before. We were given to understand that we were going to a holiday camp. We had no idea what was really going on and felt quite happy about the whole idea, especially

William and George, who had been treated very shabbily by the whole Telford family. I think we all sensed this was no temporary measure, but we were glad to be on our way, and felt a sense of adventure.

Exactly a year and a week after our father died, we left New Washington, in the company of our grandfather, and caught the bus to Newcastle. There we boarded the overnight coach to London. At the Victoria Coach Station we took another coach on to Camberley, where we alighted at a café called The Jolly Farmer. Carrying the suitcase containing all our belongings, we made our way slowly up a long, picturesque but sinister drive, bordered on either side by rhododendrons. A voiceless melancholy was beginning to overwhelm me.

Suddenly, the drive bent sharply and we beheld a huge ominous-looking building. A penetrating dream-like poison had invaded my limbs. Our grandfather was about to hand us over to the Royal Albert Orphanage.

PART II

'We are the Orphanage Boys!'

Fig 13. *The Royal Albert Orphan Asylum for Thoroughly Destitute Children.*

When my brothers and I arrived at the Royal Albert Orphanage in 1934 it was housed at Collingwood Court in the parish of Frimley Green, near Bagshot in Surrey. In 1758 the Reverend Edward Pickard had founded a working school for orphaned boys and girls in Hoxton, now in north London – though of course, in those days, Hoxton would have been a village outside London. By 1773 it had expanded to accommodate 130 children and had moved to City Road, and by 1847 numbers had grown to 240 and the school had moved once again, this time to Maitland Park, now in NW3. At the end of 1864, as a memorial to the Prince Consort, it was renamed the Royal Albert Orphan Asylum for Thoroughly Destitute Children, and transferred to Collingwood Court. Its patron was Her Majesty the Queen. The Committee which ran this institution did not intend

> to raise these children above that sphere which the providence of God has marked them out to fill, but in giving them simple education, consisting of reading, writing, and rudimentary arithmetic, and in teaching them the truths of the Bible, trust they may go forth as honest and industrious children, capable of earning their own livelihood and proving themselves useful members of society.
>
> To this end the girls are trained to become industrious and useful servants. In addition to the usual household work, they are taught washing and ironing, and especial attention is paid to their being made efficient in plain and useful needlework.

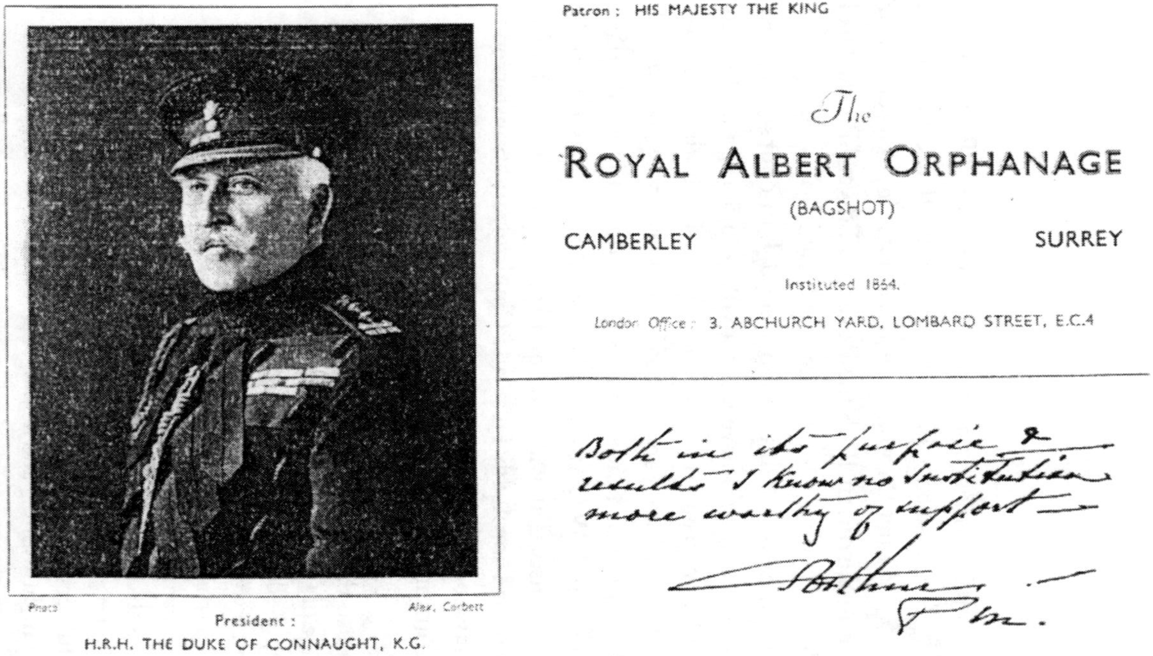

Photo Alex. Corbett

President :

H.R.H. THE DUKE OF CONNAUGHT, K.G.

Patron : HIS MAJESTY THE KING

The

ROYAL ALBERT ORPHANAGE

(BAGSHOT)

CAMBERLEY SURREY

Instituted 1864.

London Office : 3, ABCHURCH YARD, LOMBARD STREET, E.C.4

Both in its purpose & results I know no Institution more worthy of support —

Arthur. P.

Fig 14. *The Duke of Connaught was the conscientious and active president.*

The boys are taught to make themselves useful in the house, the kitchen-garden, and upon the farm, where they are gradually reclaiming a portion of the uncultivated land, but in order to meet the necessity which exists for the boys having a more extended sphere of employment, the Committee have erected workshops for teaching them an elementary knowledge of bootmaking and tailoring. ...

Children are received from all parts of the Kingdom, and are admitted between the ages of 6 and 12, the boys remaining until 14 and the girls until 15.   *The Victorian Prospectus*

By the time we got there, the place was a boys-only institution – I'm not sure when the change was introduced – admitting 'necessitous orphan boys of good character ... from any part of the Kingdom'. They were offered a 'scholastic education ... "certified efficient" under the Board of Education', and 'religious training'. Their health was 'carefully considered', and, according to the 1930s prospectus, 'the appearance and conduct of the lads would bear comparison with any school'. From the age of fourteen boys were trained 'as gardeners, carpenters, tailors, shoe repairers, bakers or office-workers, according to their suitability', and then placed in employment that would 'provide them with a good start in life'. The success of the vocational training programme was proved by the fact that 'a large proportion of those leaving the Orphanage ... made good'.

The patron was George V, and 'members of the Royal Family who were direct descendants of the Prince Consort' vice-patrons. The Duke of Connaught was the conscientious and active president.

The Second World War brought many changes. When the boys got back from their summer break in 1939 – I had left by then – they found the Signals Corps had commandeered a large part of the school, and this, so I understand, did much to reduce the harshness of the regime. The main building in which we had been housed no longer stands; it had to be pulled down when dry rot was discovered. Today, the co-educational Royal Alexandra and Albert School at Gatton Park, near Reigate in Surrey, can trace its history back nearly two-and-a-half centuries to the Reverend Edward Pickard's philanthropical foundation. So much for history.

* * *

Our grandfather rang the bell, and it was answered by a maid, who, I later discovered, was the personal maid of the superintendent and his wife. We were ushered into a vast awe-inspiring entrance hall. To the left was an enormous open fireplace – no fire was burning, despite the fact that it was November – and to the right stood a grandfather clock, and a glass case containing the spade used by Queen Victoria when she planted the giant sequoia that stood in front of the house. Our eyes were immediately drawn to a magnificent staircase, flanked by six marble pillars, at the top of which was a high arched stained-glass window.

I had never been in a place like this before, and had no idea what was happening. I felt completely helpless and gripped by the presentiment that this was somewhere I was not going to escape from so easily.

Almost immediately my brothers and I were led away to be introduced to some of the boys – or should I say inmates, as 'shades of the prison house' seemed to be closing in on us – while our grandfather had a word with the superintendent. We were brought back only when he was about to leave. Our

Fig 15. *The giant sequoia planted by Queen Victoria that stood in the front of the house.*

Fig 16. *I felt completely helpless and gripped by the presentiment that this was somewhere I was not going to escape from easily.*

parting was cold and perfunctory: no hugs, not even a handshake; and his final injunction to us, before he turned his back and walked away, was to behave.

I was eleven-and-a-half, William ten-and-a-quarter, and George eight-and-three-quarters. I cried unashamedly for a whole week. I know that my father, just a year previously, had told me to look after my two brothers, but I was inconsolable: angry, frightened, and betrayed by the very person in whom I should have been able to trust. My heart could not contain this hurt. None of the staff made the slightest attempt to comfort me, but one or two of the boys did. They may have been

through the same experience themselves and understood my grief.

William, who had quite a different character from me, took things in his own way. He had a streak of Da's violence, and I remember him being very truculent at this time. George, with his golden curls and angel looks, was the sort of child that naturally endears himself to people. Da used to take him out in the afternoons, and he always drew admiring glances.

I did not see much of William and George in those early weeks, as we were put into different classes, slept in different dormitories, and ate our meals at different tables. We even wore different uniforms. Very shortly after our arrival we were taken down to the tailor's shop, stripped of the clothes we had arrived in and issued with uniform. William and I were given red jerseys, and George a green one; all boys wore navy blue shorts, plain grey socks and boots. This made us part of the establishment, whether we liked it or not.

Our next ordeal came when we were shown the dormitories, of which there were ten. All our lives we three had slept together, mostly in the same bed; suddenly we were separated. There were four dormitories on the first floor, situated at the four corners of the house, each overlooking a different area of the grounds. They were called Victoria, Edinburgh, Connaught, and Sturdee. A bust of Admiral of the Fleet, Sir Frederick C. Doveton Sturdee, who had taken a great interest in the orphanage, stood on the mantelpiece in this dormitory, and over each bed was the name of a ship of the line which had fought in the Battle of Jutland. On the second floor the rooms were simply numbered one to four. I started out in number three, and later moved into Sturdee, where I slept under the nameplate *Inflexible*.

The youngest boys – some not more than five or six years of age – were known fondly as the midgets, and were segregated from the older ones. During the day they occupied a large attic situated at the end of a long narrow passage. There, under the eye of Miss Agnes, they played with a collection of toys, rode the two battered rocking-horses, and ate their meals at a big oval table. They slept in a dormitory on the floor below. George was a midget, but for a while William had to stay with him, as George was very distressed. What is more, no one except William and myself could understand his broad Geordie.

Soon after we arrived, I remember, a little chap aged about

five, who had been abandoned on the steps of Gateshead town hall, was admitted. He too was put under William's wing, as Miss Agnes could not understand one word he said.

The dormitories were presided over by Nurse Eileen, whose own room, together with the sick bay, was also on the top floor. Every boy in the orphanage had eyes for Nurse Eileen, as she was a handsome woman, but she was also very hard. If she heard you talking, or caught you misbehaving after lights out, then you paid the penalty. She got you up and made you stand in the cold corridor, wearing nothing but your pyjamas, until she relented and allowed you back to bed. I was to feel the wrath of Nurse Eileen on numerous occasions, as I tended to be rebellious. Not only did I have to stand in the corridor, but I was often reported to the superinten-

Fig 17. *Every boy in the orphanage had eyes for Nurse Eileen,* [left] *as she was a handsome woman, but she was also very hard.*

dent for further punishment. Her final gesture was to banish me to the dormitory reserved for bedwetters.

The place may have been called the Royal Albert Orphanage, but most of the boys did have one parent; William, George, and I were among the few real orphans in the institution, and no attempt was made to keep us together as a family. For me, those first weeks were a lonely and gloomy time. I felt haunted by the ghosts of my dead parents and my sisters. I had lost all those who were dear to me. Ganny Moffet was not dead, but she might as well have been, as we had been brutally separated from her. Our maternal grandparents had let us down completely. I even found out later that there was another orphanage quite near New Washington; but no, that wouldn't do; they had to send us to the other end of the country.

The turmoil inside me made me extremely rebellious, but the orphanage staff were indifferent to my upset; they had seen it all before, and meted out large doses of discipline and punishment.

* * *

Our day started at 6.30 a.m. with a call by the duty master or mistress. We got up, dressed, and folded up our bedding – mattress, blankets, sheets, and counterpane bearing the orphanage crest and motto: fleur-de-lys above the words 'For God and Country' – and placed it on top of the bedsprings in a basket each boy kept under his bed. We then went about our allotted chores. Four boys would remain in each dormitory to sweep the floor and polish it till it shone. Woe betide them if it did not pass muster; they would have to redo it, and, if the inspector was in a bad mood, they might be reported to the superintendent, who could always decide the offence merited a beating.

At about 7.30 we made our way to the ablution block, housed under the hall in a part known as the undercover. Here we pushed and shoved to get to the ten wash-basins and splash ourselves with cold water. Toilet arrangements were primitive and disgusting. There was a separate building, just beyond the end of the undercover, with a urinal that drained into a ditch but had no running water, one flush toilet, and nine cubicles containing wooden seats over buckets. Only the flush toilet had a door, and only male staff were allowed to use it. You were in big trouble if you were caught in there. By the end of the day you would have to push the excrement down with your foot before you could sit down. The buckets were emptied every morning by the boys who worked in the cobbler's shop – the worst chore in the orphanage. They had to wheel them a couple of hundred yards and tip the excrement into the cesspit.

Before breakfast we lined up in numerical order for inspection – I was No. 107 and William 108, but George did not have a number when we were first there, as midgets were not given one until they moved up to the senior division – before marching into the dining hall to stand in silence awaiting the entrance of the superintendent. If you had your back to what was going on, you dared not turn round, you depended on the boy opposite you to give you the nod that he had arrived.

Together we said grace, 'For what we are about to receive, may the Lord make us truly thankful,' and the Lord's Prayer, and sang the morning hymn:

> New every morning is the love
> Our wakening and uprising prove;
> Through sleep and darkness safely brought,
> Restored to life, and power, and thought.

In the evening, before we sat down to our last meal, known as tea, we sang:

> The day thou gavest, Lord, is ended,
> The darkness falls at thy behest;
> To thee our morning hymns ascended,
> Thy praise shall sanctify our rest.

The superintendent made his announcements before breakfast, and they were followed by the dreaded list of the names of boys to be punished; and the head boy, or the superintendent's current favourite, would be despatched to fetch an instrument. He had a number of these: the handle of a croquet mallet, a ruler, and a birch. He'd been a boxer in his youth, and his reflexes were very quick, so if you withdrew your hand as he was bringing down the instrument, he'd catch it with his upstroke, which hurt far more than a blow on the palm.

I seemed to receive more public chastisement than any other boy. I refused to knuckle under, and my stubborn and rebellious behaviour landed me in continuous trouble; my thighs almost always bore welts. I can't help feeling the superintendent took sadistic pleasure in this daily ritual. After he'd performed it, he swept out leaving the duty master to take over, and we could finally sit down for breakfast.

The fare never varied: we got three rounds of bread and dripping and a mug of tea; on Thursdays we also had shredded wheat, and on Sundays there was bread and margarine, with half-a-dozen dates. Urns of tea, one per table, came up in a food lift from the kitchens down below. The lift was worked by pulling a rope, and boys would compete to see who could raise or lower it with the fewest pulls. When no one was looking we used to give one another rides in this lift, a dangerous

Fig 18. Boys on the fire escape from the hall, with the windows of the undercover behind.

practice, and to be caught in the act was scarcely less so. We sat fourteen to a table, and mugs were passed up from hand to hand to be filled by the boy at the head of the table. If you were lucky, or friendly with the boy at the urn, you might get a second mug of tea.

After breakfast we enjoyed a little free time until nine o'clock, and would gravitate towards the undercover. This was an area about 30 feet by 65, light and airy as windows ran down both sides of it, with the cobbler's shop at one end, and the ablution block at the other. Beneath the windows was a bench, but there was not much room to sit down, as most of the space was taken up with wooden boxes of all shapes and sizes in which boys kept their personal belongings. Most of them had locks, and had, I think, been passed down from earlier generations of boys who had left. I acquired one, an old margarine crate, which I shared with my brothers, but we had precious little to keep in it: just our toothbrushes, and the odd pot of jam we bought ourselves. We used the undercover whenever the weather was too bad for us to go outside; we even played football there, exactly as they play five-a-side football today. It was a lively, bustling, noisy place.

At 9 o'clock we all fell into line at a blast on a whistle; the trade boys – carpenters, cobblers, tailors, bakers, farm hands, and gardeners – in one line, and the schoolboys in another. The schoolboys then marched off to their classes and the trade boys to their places of occupation. Every boy had schooling up to the age of fourteen, when he was assigned to one of the trades, or to the garden.

The schoolboys had classes until mid-day, when they were left to their own devices until lunch at 1 p.m. The trade boys worked until 12.30, when they would drift back from their departments to clean up. There would be another roll call before lunch, or dinner as it was called.

As far as I recall, the staff numbered about fifteen. There was the superintendent, Mr Paget, a character all too reminiscent of Mr Bumble, the beadle in *Oliver Twist*, and his wife, the matron. What Mrs Paget did in the way of matronly duties I have no idea, but that was her official title. On the educational side there was a senior master and a couple of other teachers. On the vocational, or trade, side there were three ladies who ran the tailor's shop, a gentleman in charge of the cobbler's shop, a gardener, and a farmer, a man who ran the bakery, and an old gentleman in charge of the carpenter's shop, who looked as if he had been there since the building was put up.

Lessons took place in three locations. Classes five, six, and seven were together in one room; classes three and four were in another; and classes one and two did their lessons in a screened off area of the assembly hall. There were just three teachers, one to each location, and the teaching was pretty basic: not much more than the three Rs.

Mr Newman – Grimp, behind his back – was the most senior master, a small, dapper, unpredictable man. He would be laughing with his class and telling jokes – generally of a smutty nature – when, for no apparent reason, he would suddenly single out a victim. He had a black, round ruler, which he would hold in his right hand, smacking it down into the palm of his left in time with his step, as he approached his prey, whom he would hit over the shoulders or rap viciously on the back of the hand.

Mr Johnson, who took classes three and four, was much more humane. The worst he would do, if you misbehaved in class, was rap your knuckles or throw a piece of chalk at you.

Unfortunately for us, he left the orphanage to go to a sanatorium. He was quite the most decent of the masters.

Mr Watson, in charge of classes one and two, had been a lieutenant in the Army Reserve, so he was a disciplinarian, but very fair. His form of punishment was to make you bend over to receive a kick in the behind. But sometimes this punishment went wrong, and he caught you between the legs.

Mr Johnson was replaced by a Mr Filkin, who soon made us realise we should have appreciated Mr Johnson more than we did. He must have been about six foot five, and was massive with it. He chastised by hitting you round the back of the head, or on the ear, with his great bare hand. I can remember hearing him roar at a boy one wet day: 'Go up to my room and fetch my colossal galoshes!' It was a brush with Mr Filkin that made William run away from the orphanage.

One morning William had an attack of hiccups in the dining room, and was told by Mr Filkin to be quiet. When he couldn't control the spasms, Mr Filkin hauled him out to stand alongside him, and with every hiccup he got Mr Filkin's elbow in the ribs. A shove too hard knocked William to the floor, where Mr Filkin pinned him down with a huge foot on his neck. At this point, I ran up and shouted, 'Leave my brother alone!' I don't remember whether I struck him in my rage, but I distracted him long enough to allow William to get up. 'Run!' I yelled, and he fled.

Of course I had not meant William to run away from the orphanage, but that is exactly what he did. And what I didn't notice at the time was that two boys followed him out and went with him.

They took off across the fields and kept going till they were well clear of Frimley Green. William claimed they went the

Fig 19. The orphanage staff

Back row l. to r.: Mr Manning (postTM), Mr Watchmar (cobbler), Mr Vivian (* 88), Mr Cox (88), Mr Crutchfield (89)

Middle row l. to r.: The Pagets' personal maid (74), Miss Paget (117), Miss Agnes Powell (78), Miss Hennessey (90), Miss Knox (postTM)

Front row l. to r.: Mr Bishop (90), Mr Newman (85), Mr Paget (85), Mrs Paget (85), Nurse Eileen (79), Miss Hanson (90), Miss Williams (90)

* The numerals in brackets indicate the text pages on which are given details of positions at the orphanage.

'wrong way', though what he meant I don't know, since the whole incident was unplanned. Had he wanted to get to London? When night fell, they had reached the outskirts of Guildford, and at 1 a.m., hungry and exhausted, they walked into a police station and told their story. In those days, in small towns and villages, a police station was often the sergeant's house, and this must have been the case, as William said a kind lady, who was perhaps the sergeant's wife, fed them, while the sergeant telephoned the orphanage. William claimed that he was the only one of the runaways to be punished, as he was judged to be the ringleader. He got six of the best, and was made to clean the main staircase for a week.

* * *

The orphanage was largely self-sufficient, thanks to the efforts of the trade boys who worked on the farm and in the kitchen garden. The farm was in the school grounds but about a quarter of a mile from the main buildings. The four or five boys who worked there were under the supervision of the farmer, Mr Vivian. He was a quiet, shy man, well liked by the boys, who took little part in the activities of the orphanage. There were about a dozen cows, which the farm boys learnt to milk, a herd of pigs – we always had home-produced pork for Christmas – and a couple of shire horses used to plough the potato fields. There was also a donkey, but he was more of a pet.

Next to the farm was the department known as the gardens, in which was an orchard, with apple, pear, plum and greengage trees, and beds where cauliflowers, carrots, parsnips, onions, and other vegetables were grown. The six or so boys who tended the gardens worked under Mr Cox, a harmless extrovert man, who used to take part in the sports activities, especially soccer and cricket, at which he rather fancied himself. He was a bit of a laugh really, and came in for a good deal of snide derision. The boys did as they were told in the garden, but otherwise took little notice of him. He could, however, report you to the superintendent. He'd make you stand for hours in front of the superintendent's garage, and, of course, if the super saw you standing there he'd enquire what you were doing and, in all probability, would punish you himself. I never saw Mr Cox strike a boy.

The bakery was run by Mr Crutchfield; and just three boys worked there. They did all the breadmaking, and cooked all our meals. When I became a trade boy, I spent most of my time in this department.

The superintendent, his wife and daughter, and the rest of the staff had their meals cooked in a separate kitchen, by a lady whose name I forget. She worked on her own, without any boys to help her. I remember she used to save stale bread and dry it out in her oven till it turned to rusk; and if for any reason you were sent to her kitchen, she'd give you a handful of rusk. Very nice!

Three boys worked in the cobbler's shop, responsible for all the boot and shoe repairs for boys and staff. And, as I have already said, they had the unpalatable task of emptying the latrines every morning.

The tailor's shop was the poor relation of the trade departments, and the boys who worked there had almost always been relegated to it as a punishment. I myself served time there. All one did was wash and darn socks and jerseys – some task for 140-odd boys! It was run by three spinsters, Miss Hanson, Miss Williams, and Miss Hennessey, who made and repaired the boys' trousers and shirts.

89

Fig 20. *The tailor's shop was the poor relation of the trade departments and the boys who worked there had almost always been relegated to it as a punishment.*

Last, but by no means least, came the carpenter's shop, the largest of the trade departments, in which eight or so boys worked under the direction of Mr Bishop. They were the elite of the trade boys, and carried out all the maintenance of the buildings: plumbing, painting, glazing, woodworking. They even serviced the boilers. For a brief period I was a member of this elite, until I had a set-to with Mr Bishop.

* * *

My first months at the orphanage were deeply traumatic, and I made almost no friends. As I have said, I'd always been one for going off on my own, and I found it very difficult adapting to having people around me twenty-four hours a day. And they, for their part, must have found me hard, if not impossible, to understand. I had a speech defect, about which my grandfather had made me very selfconscious, and in addition, I spoke broad Geordie. All anyone could get out of me, between tears, in my first week was: 'Dee ya knaas what aas's gan to dee? Aa wanna gan heyem.' But, of course, I had no home to go to.

In the end, I did make a good friend; he was a boy called Gedge, nicknamed Hoska, because of his gangling frame. He gave me the name of Cranny Lip, because every winter I used to develop a split in my bottom lip as a result of the cold. Hoska and I became inseparable; the only time we were apart was when I was involved in a team sport. He was all flailing legs and arms when he ran, and did not have the team spirit; however, we had our own sports.

Hoska was an unpretentious, dependable boy, with a very different family background from mine. He came from the Midlands and his father was still alive, but in all the time that we were in the orphanage he never had a single visitor, and I know he felt this deeply. Sometimes when we talked he would grow wistful. We'd often discuss what we'd do when we left the orphanage, and Hoska would say he thought he'd end up in the Army. I'd always been drawn to the Navy, and I persuaded him that we should sign on as boy sailors. We learnt all the semaphore flags, and I even wrote asking my grandfather's permission to join up, which, needless to say, he refused to give.

One Saturday afternoon Hoska and I wandered out of bounds down to the woods, beyond the farm, to indulge in a little of our favourite sport of tree climbing. Our game was to climb about three-quarters of the way up the first tree, which was a pine, then swing over on to the next, and so on and so on, trying to beat our record of climbing 103 trees without touching the ground. We must have been there some time, totally absorbed in what we were doing; I remember Hoska was on tree number 73 and I was on number 72, and I'd just called out the number, when I heard a voice below me saying: 'Make that your seventy-third jump to the ground, Moffett.' Just our luck! The superintendent and his wife had decided to take a stroll in the woods.

He sent us to stand outside his garage, in full view of everyone, including any member of staff who might come down the staircase in the main building. A couple of boys who came across to ask us what we'd done were spotted by Nurse Eileen, and she made them join us. There we remained all afternoon, till 6 o'clock, but that was not the end of the matter. On Monday, after the superintendent's morning announcements, we were hauled up in front of everyone and given four of the best, and I was reprimanded for being the instigator.

We hadn't just been left to stew in our own juice for a day; the reason for the twenty-four hour delay was that the superintendent did not use his cane on Sunday. I don't know if this was out of reverence for the Sabbath, or because he considered Sunday as a day of rest. If you got into trouble on a Saturday, you always hoped that by Monday it would have been forgotten – some hope!

On Sundays we all went to morning service at Saint Paul's Church, Camberley, about two miles away. We didn't have a 'Sunday best' to put on, just the regulation green or red jumpers and navy blue shorts, but we did look a little cleaner and neater than usual.

Strangely enough, in summer, the older boys wore Norfolk jackets, and shirts with stiff white collars; these were very thick and uncomfortable in hot weather. The stiff collars were made worse by the fact that they were old and frayed, and the starched edges would chafe your neck. I was reminded by an old boy, only recently, that once back in the orphanage grounds, we would take off the collars and place them around our foreheads, like eyeshades.

Few of us had any desire to attend church – the sermons were long and boring – but we were all glad of the chance to get out of our prison for a couple of hours. If we were lucky, and this depended on which master was escorting us, we were allowed to walk with a mate or pal, and to talk, provided we kept our voices down. Lots of the boys were keen car-spotters, but, remember, those were the pre-war years, when cars were still few and far between.

Now and again we would see the girls from Beaufort School, whose grounds were near ours, and this would cause a bit of a stir. We would be made to move into the road to allow the young ladies to pass by on the footpath. However, if Mr Filkin was in charge this was not enough; he'd make us cross the road and walk on the opposite side. Did this great brute think we might assault them?

Apart from the weekly visit to church, there were few opportunities for boys to get outside the grounds legally. One such was a visit to the dentist. If you needed treatment, you were accompanied by a trusted senior boy, and had to be back within a certain time. This gave you the chance to look round the Camberley shops – not that you had any money to spend. A certain amount of pilfering went on in Woolworth's, and I was at great pains to impress on William and George that they should not do any such thing. I was not above reproach, as far as shoplifting went, but I wanted to keep my brothers out of trouble.

One or two boys came from local families, and if you were taken to the dentist by one of them, you might be allowed to look in at his home, where you could be offered a drink and a bun. Such a visit never came my way.

Occasionally, a couple of masters would take a party of boys to the common, much used by the Army for training and manoeuvres. We were in Army country: Blackdown Camp Barracks, Sandhurst, and Aldershot were all within easy reach. These outings were very interesting, especially if Mr Watson, the Army Reserve Officer, was in charge. One day, he found an unexploded rifle bullet, which he took apart to show us how it worked, at the same time telling us never to attempt any such thing ourselves. An old boy, whom I met at a reunion, told me that he'd come across Mr Watson in France during the Second World War, and that by then he'd become a captain in the Army.

There were other annual outings too: we were taken to the rehearsal of the Aldershot Tattoo, and there was the trip to Littlehampton, that took place on the first Sunday in July. Littlehampton is on the Sussex coast between Bognor Regis and Worthing, and in those days it took three hours to get there from Frimley Green. There was always rather a carefree atmosphere when we piled into the coach in the morning, and as we bowled along, we sang the school songs.

> We know our manners,
> We spend our tanners,
> We are respected, wherever we may go.
> We go at riding down the tramway lines,
> Doors and windows open wide.
> We know the way to use our feet,

Fig 21. *Practising for sports day.*

Left, right, left, right, down the street.
　We are the Orphanage Boys!

Play for the Orphanage, never get beaten.
Put on your football boots, show them how to play.
When they are beaten, give them a bashing.
Put on your football boots, show them how to play.

The ball was in the centre, the referee's whistle blew.
Condie got his wits up, and away with the ball he flew.
Condie took a flying kick, and knocked the goalie flat.
　　We laid him on a stretcher,
　　Then laid him on a bed.
They rubbed his belly with a lump of jelly,
　And what do you think he said?
　　　'Rule Britannia,
　　Two tanners make a bob,

Three make one and sixpence,
    And four two bob.'

Where was the goalie, when the ball was In the net?
Sitting on the crossbar with his trousers round his neck,
                Singing:
'Collingwood, Collingwood, give us another one, do!'

When we got to Berry Hill in Sussex, the older boys had to get out and push, or the coach wouldn't have made it to the top. We'd picnic on the grass beside the road, devouring sausage rolls, bread rolls, and rock cakes, before going the last few miles.

I'd grown up beside the sea, but the English Channel is not like the North Sea, and instead of the miles of fine white sand I'd been used to, here was a beach of pebbles. We were, in fact, more interested in the town than the sea front, and we wandered about enjoying our brief moment of freedom.

We were allowed to draw out a little money for this trip, and the great question was what to spend it on. Each month our grandfather sent a postal order for one shilling and sixpence, and the money went into a joint account. I think we spent it all on things to eat. You could buy twenty oranges for sixpence, and penn'orths and ha'p'orths of sweets. There were still farthings before the War. I think we usually bought a pot of jam, which we shared between the three of us, passing it from table to table at tea time, and then locking it away in the margarine crate afterwards.

The same coach company, Whites of Camberley, used to take us once a year to Henley for a boat trip, accompanied by tea on the river. Who paid for all this? I am not sure, but I have a notion that it might have been a Miss Mueller, who lived in Camberley, and was very good to the boys of the orphanage.

She used to come once a week to teach morris dancing, driven up to the front door in her gleaming Bentley by a chauffeur wearing a peaked cap and gaiters, who would walk behind her up the steps carrying the wind-up gramophone. We strapped bells on our legs and learned how to wield batons, kerchiefs, and – best of all – swords. It was terrific fun and we enjoyed ourselves no end, though of course nobody was going to admit to this. George got very good at morris dancing and was one of the team that went to a competition in Brighton and won a medal.

Miss Mueller also gave an annual garden party for us during the summer – in fact she gave two, as there were too many of us to go all together. She organised all sorts of games competitions: ball in the bucket, egg and spoon race, wheel-barrow race, sack race, and distributed prizes to the winners. And the afternoon would be rounded off with a huge tea of sandwiches, cakes and lemonade.

* * *

Apart from such welcome breaks, my life was one of routine: bed, work, meals, and some sport. But whatever I was doing, wherever I was, I was thinking of how I might escape. My childhood in the North may have been austere, and I'd known poverty and grief, but even after we went to live with our maternal grandparents in New Washington, I retained my sense or freedom. I spent a great deal of time out and about on the street, and I had always been free to come and go as I pleased; I'd never had to live within a restricted perimeter, where certain places were designated out of bounds.

Fig 22. George got very good at morris dancing and was one of the team that went to a competition in Brighton and won a medal.

This in itself was bad enough, but it was coupled with heavy-handed discipline. Corporal punishment had been inflicted on me for as long as I could remember; Da would box my ears or thrash me, and Ganny had her tawse. I'd hardened myself to take it, and it didn't bother me too much; at least when it was finished it was over and done with. What left scars was the mental cruelty inflicted by those in whose power I found myself.

This most frequently took the form of complete indifference. What qualities, I have often wondered, did the authorities look for when recruiting staff? Not compassion, that's for sure. Did it occur to nobody that the boys in an institution like this might be in need of love and understanding? There were, as I found out later, exceptions, people who showed us some warmth and kindness, but they were a minority. The male staff who treated the boys most kindly were, on the whole, the family men. The others, who seemed to live at the orphanage and never went away even at Christmas, may, for all I know, have been orphans themselves, victims of a harsh, loveless upbringing. I have already said that when I arrived at the orphanage I cried for a week, and the only words or comfort I received came from one or two of the boys. The superintendent must have known our family circumstances, but not a gesture did he make to help us settle in. When I was feeling down, or had hurt myself, it would have been so comforting to have a shoulder to cry on, but none of the women staff seemed to be approachable.

My friend Hoska felt his lack of visits keenly, and I know how it was, because in all our time at the orphanage we had only one visitor. An officer from the New Washington Corps of the Salvation Army, a Captain Paul, happened to be in the area,

Fig 23. *Big Moffett with billiard cue, and friends.*

and he called by one day to ask after us, but he brought us nothing, did not ask us out, and left almost as soon as he'd shaken us by the hand. Most boys did receive visits, and had a home and at least one parent. It was hard for those not so fortunate, and no one tried to make it up to the more deprived children.

I hated having to stand on the cold landing for talking in the dormitory, but when I was sent to the bedwetters' dormitory as an additional punishment for my rebelliousness, I had to suffer the taunts and ridicule of staff and boys. In those days, bedwetting was seen as something shameful; now we know it is a sign that a child is distressed or upset, but nobody tried to help the poor unfortunates who had this problem.

Everyone needs the comfort and reassurance that a cuddle or a hug can give — orphans, possibly, more than most — but practically the only physical contact we had with staff was through punishment. However, having said that, I think I should add that there was no sexual abuse of boys by staff. This is worth saying, as we read so much nowadays of the prevalence of sexual abuse in children's homes.

Nor was bullying much of a problem either. There was a boy called Chapman, who might be said to have had a gang, but it didn't amount to much; and when there was an instance of bullying, the boys tended to deal with it themselves, and the perpetrator would be sent to Coventry. If anyone roughed up George or William, one of their friends would tip Big Moffett the wink, and I'd go and sort things out. The name Big Moffett was nothing to do with my size – in fact, I'm on the short side – it merely indicated that I was the oldest brother.

*　　*　　*

The 1930s prospectus may have boasted that 'The health of the boys is carefully considered', but our diet left much to be desired. I have described the unvarying breakfast; the 6 p.m. tea, the last meal of the day, was equally unvarying and almost identical: three slices of bread and margarine, and a mug of cocoa. On Thursday nights there was a dessertspoonful of golden syrup to go with the bread-and-scrape, and on Sundays we got a rock-bun; but it's easy to see why we spent our precious pocket-money on pots of jam. For a while William was one of the team that spread the margarine on the bread, and he'd see to it that Tom's three slices had a little extra marg' on them. He could do this because we had our regular places in the dining room, and the food was put out on individual plates. Miss Hennessey, from the tailor's shop, was in charge of this operation, and I think she grew quite attached to William and sympathised with his volatile nature.

The uniformity of the weekly lunchtime menu was such that I can still recall it:

> Monday : Herrings in tomato sauce. Bread pudding.
> Tuesday : Meat pie, potatoes and vegetables.
> Wednesday: Stew, ugh!
> Thursday : Meat pudding, potatoes and vegetables.
> Friday : Toad in the hole, known always as Micky Fynn.
> Saturday : Soup.
> Sunday : Corned beef, beetroot and potatoes. Boiled rice pudding.

For most of the first ten years of my life I had been hungry, and I have admitted that I was always on the scrounge for things to eat, and even resorted to pinching from the market stalls. Then there was the year we stayed in New Washington; if we did not get the same food as the rest of the family, at least we always had enough to eat. At the orphanage, I found myself hungry once again.

It was on a Tuesday, after the mid-day meal, that a train of events started which was to lead to one of the most memorable escapades in my young life. Three of us from my table, who were still hungry, decided we would pay a visit to the superintendent and complain. We set out on a rather tortuous route for his private quarters. Using the rear entrance to the building – the only one that boys were allowed to use – we crossed the room where we changed from our outdoor boots into plimsoles, then climbed an iron spiral staircase, at the top of which was a narrow passage, wide enough for only one person to pass at a time, leading to the main landing where the superintendent's private quarters were.

I found myself at the head of the delegation, and knocked

boldly on his sitting room door. We were answered by the superintendent himself, looking none too pleased to see us. Had we, I wonder, disturbed his afternoon nap? The other two had lost their tongues, so it was left to me to do the talking. He heard me out, and then said that if we hadn't had enough to eat, we could ask for some dry bread. I said something to the effect that we got that for breakfast and tea, and asked why we couldn't have more meat. This was too much for him, and he grabbed one of his canes, which he kept hanging just inside the door. I turned tail – my two companions had already fled – and almost literally flew down the narrow passage. This one-time boxer had fast reflexes; he was after me and managed to land a couple of blows on the back of my legs before I got to the head of the spiral staircase. As I slowed down and turned to negotiate this, he caught me again with his cane. I stumbled and fell headfirst, and had the staircase not been spiral, I would have fallen from top to bottom; as it was, I must have fallen down about six steps. I have said that the superintendent bore more than a passing resemblance to Mr Bumble in *Oliver Twist*; I now knew, from personal experience, what could happen to boys who ask for 'more'.

This clinched things. I and my two associates – I call them associates rather than friends, for I was in league with them only for a short time – decided we would run away. They were both about my age: 'Dinger' Bell, who came from London and was not the brightest of lads, and Bob Straughan, a more canny boy and a fellow northerner. We didn't spend weeks laying our plans, in fact, such was our naiveté and lack of preparation that we did not even think to take any food with us.

We decided to make our escape on a Sunday afternoon,

immediately after the 3 o'clock roll call. In the middle of the afternoon, we were summoned by a whistle to assemble and answer to our numbers, and having done this, we could go back to whatever we were doing until the next roll call at 6 p.m. before tea. There would be three hours before we would be missed.

We set off across the playing field, keeping close to the rhododendrons bordering the drive and stopping every now and then to give the impression to anyone who might have been watching that we were playing. We were careful not to be seen making a beeline for the woods, which were out of bounds. We crossed the woods, crossed the football pitch and another small field and reached the main road to Frimley Green, now the A33.

We walked a short way along this road – high-risk territory since our uniforms would have made us instantly recognisable – then turned in behind a row of houses and the local garage until we reached the railway cutting. We slid down the embankment, crossed the line, climbed up the other side and crossed the road to Camberley. We were now on the open common; there was heather and bracken as far as the eye could see. We pushed on quite deeply into the common till we were no longer visible from the road, and then turned, as we thought, towards London.

On we trudged, mile upon mile, having no idea of what time it was or how far we had come. After what seemed like hours, we decided we'd better find a main road, as we did not want to be stranded on the common after dark. We discovered we had got beyond Bagshot, which was a good thing as the RAO was known there, and were on the outskirts of Sunningdale.

As we walked along on the greensward, we looked with

awe at the aristocratic world about us. We saw large detached houses standing in well-tended gardens and with cars parked in the drive, signposts to places I had always thought of with reverence, names to be whispered: Virginia Water, Egham, Ascot. We watched carefree families enjoying a Sunday outing, and amused ourselves carspotting.

At one point we found a thermos flask on the grass, obviously left behind by picnickers. It was three-quarters full of tea, without milk or sugar. We each took a sip; we had drunk nothing for hours, and it was like nectar. On further tasting, however, we decided it was disgusting, so tipped out the tea but saved the flask. Alas, one of my companions dropped it and the glass lining shattered.

I'm not sure now exactly when this adventure took place, but I think it was mid to late September. Night was beginning to fall, and our troubles were about to begin. Where were we going to sleep? We were very weary, and the seeds of doubt were beginning to sprout in our minds. Had this been such a good idea after all? Yes, we decided; anything was better than being locked away in that prison.

We came to a sort of copse beside the main road – I think we'd reached Egham – and this seemed a good place to doss down for the night. There was nothing but leaves to lie on, and we had one jacket between the three of us. We selected a suitable spot under a big tree and settled down.

We wondered what would be happening back at the orphanage, and we agreed we'd have to be very wary the next day as, obviously, the police would have been alerted, though we had no idea how far their dragnet would extend. My thoughts turned to William and George. What were they thinking? How were they coping with the grilling they were surely getting? No one was going to believe that they knew nothing of our plans. I learnt afterwards that William was beaten in an attempt to extract information from him.

Eventually we fell asleep from sheer exhaustion. I don't know how long we'd been asleep before it started to rain, and we were woken by heavy drops falling from the leaves above. We found we were pretty wet. This made us decide we'd better get moving, despite the fact that it was still quite dark, and there was no sign of life stirring.

We had not gone far along the road when we came to a cycle shop, behind which, in a yard, there seemed to be a cycle store. With a bicycle each we would make much better headway. No one seemed to be about, so we climbed over the gate and reconnoitred. In point of fact, there were only three bicycles there, one of which was minus the saddle, so we had no choice to make. Luckily, the gate we had climbed over was secured only with bolts, otherwise we'd have had trouble getting out with our machines.

We pedalled off into the darkness, without lights, of course, but dawn was beginning to break. Again, I have no notion of the distance we covered, but we seemed to make good progress, and at one point we crossed a long bridge over a wide river. Some time between ten and eleven o'clock in the morning we decided to look for a cup of tea, and to try find out where we were. Dinger swore we were almost in London. 'I should know,' he said, 'me being a Londoner.'

We had about one shilling and sixpence between us, so when we came to what looked like a restaurant set a little way back off the road, we propped our bikes against the kerb and tried the door, which was round the side of the building. The place appeared to be shut, so we returned to our bikes and had a conference about what to do. We'd go to the back of the building and see if anyone was about.

This was a foozle; we should have got straight back on our bikes and looked for another place, for when we returned to the kerb the second time, a police car – a rare sight in those days – had pulled up, and two policemen were standing waiting for us. They asked what we were up to, and we told them we were looking for a cup of tea. Didn't we know the place was closed? No. If we'd known that, we wouldn't have stopped.

They must have guessed we were not local boys, and decided to question us more closely. We insisted we were just out for a bicycle ride, but they looked at the machine without a saddle and weren't about to believe that. We realised the cat was out of the bag, and that we had better come clean. We told them we'd run away from the Royal Albert Orphanage, but they'd never heard of the place, so I don't think they believed us. We were bundled into the police car and taken to Wood Green police station. So we'd made it to London after all.

At the police house a very motherly lady appeared and offered us a cup of tea – welcome indeed, as it was getting on for twenty-four hours since we'd had a proper drink. Then she sat us down to a hot meal, the like of which we had not seen for a very long time. While we were eating, the policemen questioned us: Why had we absconded? How had we managed to do so? And we certainly didn't paint a very rosy picture of the orphanage and its staff. I have no idea how much notice they took of our complaints; after all, in those days, little boys in orphanages were just one more social problem to be swept under the carpet. As far as they were concerned, the most serious thing we had done was to steal the three bicycles.

They got in touch with the orphanage, checked on our story,

and informed them that the fugitives had been apprehended; they then drove us back. Our two captors had become very friendly – who knows, they may have had boys of their own – and I think they begun to be sympathetic to our plight.

We knew we would be punished, but little did we realise what we were in for. The superintendent didn't see our running away as an escapade, or as an act of bravado or desperation; he took it as a personal slight. We were beaten and paraded in front of the whole community, staff and boys, belittled, ridiculed, and accused of tarnishing the reputation of the orphanage. He even implicated my two brothers, who had had nothing whatsoever to do with the affair. We then received six more lashes.

I imagined that that was the end of the matter, as for a month or so things more or less got back to normal, but I had reckoned without the tenacity of the Law. A summons came for us to appear in court in Egham to answer charges of stealing three bicycles, and we were driven over there by a grim-faced superintendent in his Morris 12, registration EPD 734 – why do I remember this minute, irrelevant detail?

The proceedings were very formal: the court ushers were stiff and cold, and there was certainly no kind lady with cups of tea. One of the policemen who had picked us up in Wood Green was there to give evidence. The magistrates put us on probation for two years; I wonder if they had any idea what had driven us to run away from the orphanage.

I doubt that this trivial matter merited even a line in the local press, but the superintendent took it very seriously indeed: we had brought public disgrace on the Royal Albert Orphanage. As soon as we got back we were marched down to the cobbler's shop, and Mr Nun, who used to cut the boys' hair, was instructed to shave our heads. We were made to take off our daytime clothes, which were then confiscated for the duration, and put on our pyjamas. We'd been convicted, so we were going to be made to look like convicts. We were then paraded in front of the school, and the superintendent announced that we were to be segregated for a month, and that anyone caught trying to make contact with us would be punished.

We were locked up in an attic dormitory, where our meals were delivered by a senior boy, who'd obviously had instructions not to linger and chat. During all this time I was allowed no contact with my brothers; in fact, we didn't even set eyes on any of the other boys, as the room was high up and at the remotest corner of the building.

One thing we did see, however, was the burning of Crystal Palace. We were looking out of our window one night, when we saw an extraordinary glow on the distant skyline, a sort of miniature aurora borealis, that lit up the whole sky. We gazed fascinated, having no idea what it could be, and only found out later by chance. The boy who brought up our dinner forgot the water jug, and inadvertently left the door unlocked while he went to fetch it. Dinger Bell slipped out and into a master's room, where he picked up an old newspaper. The Palace, which had been built to celebrate the Great Exhibition of 1851, had been burnt to the ground on the night of 30 November 1936. We must have been some thirty-five miles away as the crow flies, and I understand the glow in the sky could be seen from as far off as Brighton.

* * *

Once we'd served our term of incarceration in the attic, we

were still branded as criminals, but we were allowed to return to lessons and duties. One of the first things I had to do was face my brothers, who had been given a very rough time as a result of my actions. This had even continued after we had been brought back to the orphanage and punished.

They'd been made to stand outside the superintendent's office for hours at a time, and were periodically taken in for questioning about our escape. They were simply not believed when they swore that they knew nothing at all about the whole affair. So harshly were they treated that George blurted out that he wished we'd taken him with us, and that we'd never been caught. For this he was beaten, and the sheer injustice of it enraged me.

Our father, on his deathbed, had bade me look after my brothers – 'Ye a gan a be the fether noo' – instructions I was not likely to forget. But I was still too upset by all we had been through in our early lives, too hurt, rebellious and bewildered to be able to think of them, and I'm afraid to say that in our early years at the orphanage it can't have made life easier for them having me as their older brother. I got into a lot of trouble, and all I could do was impress upon them to keep themselves out of scrapes – 'Do as I say, not as I do.' This worked up to a point, but William was very strong willed and frequently defied me. He was not above being heavy-handed with George, and when I tackled him about this on one occasion, he threw a brick at me, catching me squarely on the forehead. In point of fact though, we didn't see all that much of one another; we slept in different dormitories, were in different classes, and sat at different tables for our meals. Nevertheless, I think I can say that there was a strong bond between us.

Life got back to some sort of normality. I was far from

happy, and my rebellious spirit had not been broken, but I did make a bit of an effort to settle down. What I still found hard to bear was the feeling of not being wanted by anyone, of having been rejected and abandoned by my family.

Six months or so after we ran away I turned fourteen, stopped my schooling and became a trade boy. I'd always had a strong desire to enter the carpenter's shop, and to my great surprise my wish was granted. I felt grown up and very proud the first time I lined up with the other trade boys. There were eight of us in this shop, run by Mr Bishop, and the senior boy assigned me to a bench, and issued each of the newcomers with a set of tools, and an apron with large pockets for keeping our tools in. I was the youngest of the new recruits so found myself at the last bench in the farthest corner of the workshop; it had a broken vice and my tools had seen better days, but who was I to complain? I was just happy to be a member of this elite corps.

Alas, I was not to become one of Mr Bishop's favourites. I seemed prone to create disturbances, and things came to a head after only four months, at the end of July, as we were making preparations for the summer camp.

Those boys who had no relatives to return to spent the month of August under canvas, enjoying a break from the daily routine, and a little more freedom than usual. The camp was some distance from the main buildings, and Mr Bishop and Mr Cox, who both lived with their families in cottages in the school grounds, kept an eye on things, but I think the boys more or less ran the ran the camp themselves.

We'd pitched the bell tents and had started to erect the marquee. This had a heavy frame consisting of two upright poles and a crossbar, rather like a set of goal posts, and it had

Fig 24. *I'd always had a strong desire to enter the carpenter's shop.*

to be pulled by guys. Two boys held each of the uprights steady and four other boys pulled on the guys. Once it had been raised, two of the boys on the guys had to secure the frame in position, which meant leaving only a single boy bearing half the weight of frame. I was just not big enough to hold it steady, and the rope began to slip through my fingers. The structure listed and the other boys had to let down their side very quickly with the risk of splitting the crossbar. All the while old man Bishop was ranting and raving, and when the whole thing crashed to the ground he came up to me and said, 'Stop picking your nose, and go and get a sickle. You can start cutting those bushes over there!' My indignation boiled over. I couldn't help it if I wasn't heavy enough to anchor the guy; he should have been supervising this operation properly. I tore off my apron, threw it at him, and told him he could cut the bushes himself. Then I turned to run away, but where was there to go to?

After that Mr Bishop was not having me back, and anyway I had no desire to return. Once more I was to be punished for my deplorable conduct. My name was read out after the superintendent's morning announcements, and all the staff had been especially summoned to witness my humiliation. I received six lashes on my hands and four on my bottom, and it took all the willpower I could muster to hold back the tears of anger, tears of pain. In addition, I was relegated to the tailor's shop for an indefinite period.

* * *

There were three of us in the tailor's shop; I don't know why the other two had been sent there. One was the boy Chapman, with whom I didn't get on very well. As I've said, he had a small gang of followers, who, although they weren't bullies, were rather an intimidating bunch, wandering about using spoiling tactics. The other was my pal, Hoska, and this was certainly a redeeming feature. I can only think he was in the tailor's shop because he was completely unambitious, and didn't seem to mind what he did. Miss Hanson was in charge and her two assistants were Miss Williams and Miss Hennessey.

The ladies made all the uniform shirts and shorts; and, of course, there was an awful lot of mending to do. Our job was to look after the socks. These were changed once a week, on Fridays after lunch. We'd collect the dirty socks and spend the afternoon washing them. In summer we'd hang them up to dry outside, in winter we took them to the boiler room. One day when we were hanging up the socks in the boiler room, Miss Hennessey, who'd climbed on to a chair to reach the line, fell down when the chair collapsed under her. Needless to say, we all laughed, but I was the only one she happened to see laughing. I was castigated strongly, and she threatened to report me to the superintendent, but in the end thought better of it – thank goodness! On Monday morning we had the job of pairing the socks and – worst of all – darning them; some had holes you could put your fist through. I soon learnt to darn, and still pride myself on my skill with wool and needle.

Mention of the boiler house reminds me of the boy whose job it was to keep the boilers stoked and clinkered. His name was 'Ginger' Bridges, and he was an affable character, who took quite a few of the younger boys under his wing. With members of staff, however, he could be truculent, resisting the harsh discipline, but for some reason he was allowed to go his own way; I dare say that was why he was given the job with the boilers.

We didn't get to enjoy much of the hot water Ginger produced; there were precious few radiators, and in the mornings we had to wash in cold water, but Friday night was bath night for the whole school. This weekly ritual was presided over by the duty master in the case of the bigger boys, and by Miss Williams for the midgets. The bathrooms were located at either end of the corridors where the dormitories were. The large cast-iron baths held two boys at a time, and, as there were sixteen to a dormitory, the water was neither hot nor clear by the time the last pair got into it. I remember we washed ourselves with big bars of yellow carbolic soap; it had a clean astringent smell that I still love. Last boy out of the bathroom had the job of scouring the tub with green Monkey Brand paste.

The washers-up also used hot water, but their chore was still a most unpopular one. In those pre-detergent days you ran a sinkful of water, then jiggled a small wire basket containing the ends of old bars of soap in the water, and this was supposed to cut the grease. The plate scrapings went into a 'pig bucket' that was sent down to the farm.

In the end Ginger Bridges went too far; he fell foul of the authorities and was expelled. Rumour had it that he and a boy named Barber had drilled a spy hole through a ceiling and had seen two members of staff 'misbehaving'. What exactly happened, I can't say, as, naturally, the matter was hushed up. All I know for certain is that Ginger and Barber were sent packing.

Although I was none too happy at being relegated to the tailor's shop, I see now that it did me a lot of good. Firstly, I was working with a friend, and, once I had got over my initial feeling of humiliation, I began to get on with the ladies in charge, especially Miss Hanson and Miss Williams, who were good to me. This was the first kindness any member of staff had shown me, and I responded. I started to think about my behaviour, and my attitude to life in general.

I hadn't long been in the tailor's shop when I was given the job of looking after the ladies' rest room. I had to keep it clean and tidy, and, in winter, clear the grate and light a fire. I made a special effort to do my chores when Miss Williams would be there on her day off, for she was not above making small demonstrations of favour, and would sometimes produce a few sweets or a bar of chocolate. I responded eagerly and would occasionally steal a few flowers from the garden to brighten up the room for her. In fact, I developed what I can only describe as affectionate feelings for her, which I believe were reciprocated – perhaps she too had been starved of love. It was all, I hasten to add, completely innocent, and Miss Williams was not even my favourite member of staff. This was Miss Hanson, who ran the tailor's shop, and was an older, more motherly woman. She was always quietly spoken – she had no need to raise her voice to assert her authority – and commanded great respect. She was the first person to encourage me to reform and settle down. She once had occasion to report me to the superintendent. I'd polished the dormitory floor and she didn't consider the job had been done properly; I argued my case with her and it was this that merited the referral. But what hurt more than the four lashes I received was the fact that she'd reported me.

When I'd spent three months or so in the tailor's shop, the superintendent, who used to pay a daily visit and stand warming his behind in front of the fire, turned one morning to the ladies and asked, 'Do you know who is the most improved boy in the school?' I think we must all have stopped working and stared at him. 'It's our Tom, over there', he said. I was thunderstruck, not only at this announcement, but also at his using my Christian name. He went on to say that because of my improvement he was going to transfer me from the tailor's shop at the end of the week.

Much to my surprise, and I think to the surprise of every-one in the orphanage, the superintendent turned me over to his daughter. This lady, Miss Margaret Paget, was a bit of mys-tery to us; none of us knew what she did. Every weekday morning her father used to drive her somewhere; and we all assumed she was a teacher, though I now believe she was attending Royal Holloway College. She had nothing to do with the running of the orphanage, and never spoke to any of the boys, but she did look after the garden and lawns in front of the main building, and very neat she kept them. I was to be her part-time assistant.

Naturally, I was apprehensive about close involvement with a member of the Paget family, but she turned out to be not at all the dragon I'd been expecting, and we got on very well. She was extremely kind, in an aloof sort of way, and I learnt a lot from her about people and their attitudes. She, too, did a great deal to help me settle down and reform my ways.

I had to take a lot of stick from the boys, who were begin-ning to call me 'teacher's pet', but that didn't worry me too much, as for the first time since I'd arrived at the orphanage I was happy. People were showing an interest in me, treating me kindly, and I blossomed.

I had a narrow escape one day, as we were clearing rubbish from behind the gazebo at the end of the lawn. I'd lifted an old tea-chest and was about to pick up what I thought was a bundle of dirty cotton wool, when Miss Margaret shouted at me not to touch it. She made me run for a bottle of eucalyptus oil from the nurse, which she proceeded to pour over the strange object. I'd been about to pick up a wasps' nest.

We'd take breaks from work in the gazebo, and, over a cup of tea or glass of orange squash, Miss Margaret would ask me about my ambitions and hopes for the future. It was she, I believe, who was responsible for my being given a part-time job outside the orphanage that was to shape the course of my life. I was sent to the house of people who, I assume, must have been friends of hers, to work as a trainee butler.

They lived a little way up the Frimley Road, and I was trusted to walk there on my own. This in itself was a huge privilege, but in addition, from the first moment, I loved the work and the atmosphere. The lady of the house, madam – oddly enough I do not recall her name – was rather austere, but kind; she would be at the tradesmen's entrance to greet me when I arrived once a week in the morning, and would lead me into the kitchen to join the butler.

His name was Rupert, but of course I never addressed him by it; he was my boss, so to me he was 'sir'. I can't say what age he was, but he seemed rather old, as he had grey hair; he moved with a slow, shuffling walk, and went about his work in a measured, deliberate way. I'd never been in a house like this before, and had to be shown how to do everything; but he explained in a patient, businesslike way, and, despite being very particular, never put me down or belittled me.

I set to with a will, cleaning the silver, polishing glasses, and scouring saucepans. My favourite gadget was the machine that sharpened and polished the steel knife blades. They'd be all grey and dull when you stuck them into slots in a kind of drum, but after a couple of turns of the handle, the blades would come out sharp and shining.

I never once saw the gentleman of the house – he'd left for the City before I arrived, and returned only in the evening – but the butler would explain about greeting him with his apéritif when he got home, and tell me what wines he would be serving with dinner. I drank it all in, hung on his every word. Something, I can't say exactly what it was, pleased me about the atmosphere; I really loved being there.

When it was time for me to return to the orphanage, madam would appear in the kitchen and give me my wages: half-a-crown for a morning's work – this was *real* money. I couldn't help wondering what my dear mother would have thought, if she'd been able to see me; her boy from the back streets of South Shields working in this big house, and making a good job of it. She'd have been astonished and so proud.

I realise now that this was not a large or grand establishment. The house stood in its own grounds and the family employed a butler, cook, gardener, and maid; but this was nothing unusual for a middleclass family before the Second World War, when wages were low, and domestic service made up a very big segment of the labour market.

I stayed for a year, during which time I gained a lot of insight, and developed such a taste for the job that I wanted to prepare for the catering trade. Miss Margaret must have spoken to her father about me, as before long he summoned me to his room for a talk. He complimented me on my reformed behaviour and, when he asked me what trade I'd like to learn, I promptly opted for the bakery. The following Monday, with Miss Margaret's blessing, this was where I went.

* * *

Mr Crutchfield, who ran the bakery, was a simple, kindly, family man – very different from all the other masters – who lived with his wife and ten-year-old son in a small cottage on the edge of the grounds, and took no part in the social life of the orphanage. He had the habit of standing with his hands on his hips and shaking his right knee in a nervous manner when talking to you. I've no doubt he knew all about my past history, and I wondered how we'd get on. I needn't have worried; there was a good atmosphere in the bakery, and I fitted right in. We were encouraged to talk and say what we thought, without fear of being reported to the superintendent. A good deal of leg-pulling went on, and Mr Crutchfield could stand a joke against himself, as long as we knew when we'd gone far enough.

We made bread twice a week, on Mondays and Thursdays. There were no automatic mixers or synthetic rising agents; we did it all the old-fashioned way, kneading by hand, learning how long to let the dough rise, when to knock it back, and how to mould it for the tins, or shape it into bloomers and cottage loaves. The oven was extremely primitive. Our first task, on coming into the bakery in the morning, was to dispose of the prisoners trapped in the large earthenware crock that had been left overnight below the oven door. The place teemed with cockroaches, and those that fell into the crock could not get out and were thrown to matron's chickens. Then we made a fire in the oven, and when the oven had reached the right temperature we raked the fire out, washed down the oven with a cloth on the end of a pole before putting in the loaves with a peel – a contraption shaped somewhat like an oar or paddle – and sealing the oven. The timing had to be just right.

We made all the meals for the boys, so what we learnt was very basic institutional cookery. We made pastry for the meat pies and prepared the vegetables. I wish I could say that the food improved after I joined the bakery, but the truth is that you can't produce good food without good ingredients. Bread and butter pudding, in which crustless slices of white bread, interlayered with currants and sultanas, are baked in a creamy egg custard, bears no resemblance to bread pudding orphanage style. We soaked stale bread in a mixture of milk and water, squeezed it out, added a little dried fruit, and put it in the oven in large tins.

The potatoes were peeled by boys who had been sent for punishment by a duty master, but just occasionally we'd have a volunteer potato peeler, who hoped to earn himself a slice of bread or a stale rock bun. I stopped being perpetually hungry once I started in the bakery, as we were able to nibble all day long.

When I'd been in the bakery for about six months, the senior boy, by the name of Balch, who like me had two younger brothers, 'Smiler' and 'Smudge', left. Mr Crutchfield moved me up, not to second place, but to joint senior, as the boy who had been number two was only a few weeks older than me, and he thought we should be able to work together as a team. Before long, however, I was made senior boy, which was a great boost to my morale. Smiler joined us shortly after Balch senior left, and he became quite a pally with me and Hoska, who, by this time was working as a gardener. Smiler and I were both picked for the cricket team, so we spent a lot of time in each other's company.

Whit Monday was Old Boys' Day, and in the afternoon there would be a cricket match; but I remember less about any matches I played in than I do about a game called 'a penny on the wicket', in which old boys would place a penny on the stumps and we tried our skill bowling to knock it off and keep the penny .

In fine weather, when we were not working or involved in team practice, we were free to wander all over the grounds. We had plenty of space as there was a five-acre playing field, and behind a disused scout hut a strip of land had been divided into plots for boys to have their own gardens. William, George and I eventually acquired a plot, but never managed to do much with it, since the only seeds we had to plant were those we could scrounge from other boys. Most of our free time was spent sitting under an enormous majestic beech tree, chatting, reading, or just watching what was going on around us. I longed to get my nose into a book, but the orphanage had no library when I was there. Boys with visitors received comics; and well-thumbed copies of *Wizard*, *Hotspur*, *Film Fun*, *Magnet*, *Bubbles*, and *Chips* were passed from hand to eager hand. We swapped cigarette cards, but as there were no grown-ups to cadge new ones off, our meagre collections never grew. William, George, and I had virtually no personal possessions; I'd had to leave behind the beautiful working crane I received on my first Christmas in New Washington.

We had to write a monthly letter to our grandfather. We'd thank him for the one-and-sixpenny postal order, and rack our brains for something to say as there was not much variation in our lives, and I was not going to tell him about the trouble I got into. All boys' mail, in and out, was censored by the staff, and I can remember one lad having a letter from his father soaked in Eusol disinfectant, as it had mentioned a chickenpox epidemic.

By now I was one of the seniors, and had calmed down a lot. I'd stopped being suspicious of anyone who tried to approach me, I even realised that some members of staff were actually trying to help me, and I was much more easy-going with the other boys. Perhaps also I was trying to set an example to William and George, who for a long time had been penalised as a result of my recalcitrant behaviour. I was still not a model youngster, but my name was put forward for the gold medal awarded annually to the most popular boy. I'm told I failed to win it by one vote.

When I look back on my five-and-a-quarter years at the orphanage, I think the most important thing I learnt was toleration. I'd been thrown in with a lot of boys who'd been through many of the trials and tribulations I'd suffered, and we all had to get on together. The educational standard was lamentably low, but we were grounded in the three Rs, and the very regularity of the routine gave our lives a kind of stability.

* * *

I may have given the impression that, apart from day trips, we never left the orphanage at all, but this was not so; every year we returned to New Washington for the whole of August. A master would accompany us to King's Cross station and put us on to the Newcastle train. The fare, I remember, was £1.0s.6d each.

The first time we went we were terrifically excited, but our optimism was short-lived. The truth was that we were not wanted in our grandparents' house, and nothing was done to disguise this fact. We still had our meals after the rest of the family, and Lillian was her old unpredictable self. My nose was put out of joint when I discovered that she had taken over my job on the market crockery stall, but of course I can see the logic of that.

George had a particularly unpleasant incident with Grandma when he returned one August after I'd gone out into the world. She was convinced someone was pilfering food, and accused him. He swore he was innocent – as indeed he was – and at the same time he had a good idea who the culprit was, but didn't dare voice his thoughts. Grandma set out to catch him. She baked a cake to which she added a hefty measure of disinfectant, and left this in a prominent place on the larder shelf. The next day her son John was taken violently ill with stomach cramps and vomiting, and the doctor was called in. When the truth then came out, needless to say, she did not apologise to George.

I'm convinced that it was our stepgrandmother who was instrumental in our being sent to the orphanage. Granddad may have appeared to rule the roost but, as I've said, he always deferred to her. By the end of the month we knew we had outstayed our welcome, and were glad enough to be returning to the orphanage. I know this may sound unlikely, in view of all I have said about the place, but it was preferable to the chilly atmosphere in our grandparents' house.

All boys, whether or not they had any family, spent Christmas at the orphanage. For several days beforehand we were busy making holly chains. The gardeners brought in branches of holly, and we stripped off the leaves and berries, attached them to strings with needle and cotton – a prickly, fiddling job – and strung them round the assembly hall and the main entrance hall. The atmosphere grew less oppressive as preparations got under way; lessons had stopped for the school-boys, though the trade boys kept on at their tasks, and there was the occasional outing, like the one I mentioned to the common.

We didn't go to church on Christmas morning, but had a school service with lots of carols. For lunch there was roast pork with crackling, from the pigs looked after by Mr Vivian and the farm boys, roast potatoes, vegetables, and Christmas pudding. Nobody was reprimanded for making too much noise.

In the afternoon we crowded into the assembly room and took our places round the sides for present-giving. Every boy got something, and Colonel Foley, a committee member, and Miss Mueller distributed the parcels. If a boy's family had sent something, that was his lot; for those with nothing, local business people provided a gift. Granddad cannily sent nothing for us in time for Christmas, so we would each receive one of the mediocre toys from local philanthropists, but after Christmas a Cadbury's selection box would arrive.

On Christmas night the older boys were invited into the hall to dance with members of staff. Mr Newman would pound out waltzes, quicksteps, and foxtrots on the piano, and oddly-matched couples would glide self-consciously around the floor. Every boy wanted to dance with Miss Williams, for I think we were all a little in love with her. Come Boxing Day it was all over, and the old routine was resumed.

In July 1938 I attended my last prize day. Excitement had

been building up for some time, and I was on tenterhooks to know if I was going to be awarded a prize. I knew I should get something, as I had come second in the mile race, but there were other prizes too, for conduct and progress.

On the great day, we were all neatly togged out in clean uniform, and formed ourselves into a guard of honour for the Duke of Connaught to make his inspection.

Prize-giving took place in the assembly hall, and I received two: a leather purse for my performance in the mile race, and – to my surprise and pleasure – a pocket watch for being a good and helpful head boy in the bakery.

I was soon to turn sixteen and the question of my future had to be settled. It was clear that my grandfather did not want me back in the North near his family, and I certainly had no desire to return there. Uncle Billie, my mother's brother, grandfather's son by his first wife, was now married and living in Cambridge. He was one of the few members of my family I was fond of, and negotiations were opened on my behalf with him. He found me a place in a large bakery and catering establishment in Cambridge, and it was agreed I should live with him.

I was taken to an outfitter in Camberley and bought a complete set of new clothes. For the first time in my life I put on long trousers, and a tie which I had to learn to knot. Everything, I recall, was brown: suit, shirt, tie and trilby.

On 13 January 1939, I think I can truly say that my feelings were in as great a state of turmoil as they were the day I arrived at the Royal Albert Orphanage. I was about to say goodbye to William and George, from whom I'd never been separated before, and go out into the wide world. To say that I was ignorant would be an understatement: we never set eyes on a newspaper – the only one I saw in the whole of my time at the orphanage was the one Dinger Bell chanced to get hold of when we were shut up in the attic – nor listened to the wireless, except on one occasion in 1937, when we were allowed to gather round the radiogram for the commentary on the Cup Final between Sunderland and Preston North End.

I didn't know what I was going to say to William and George. I feel things very deeply, and I had a lump in my throat, but we're not a demonstrative family. In the end, I think I just mumbled something about being good boys, and turned away. With a coach ticket to Cambridge via London in my pocket, I walked down the majestic drive for the last time, through the gates, and out into a world, which – little did I know it – was on the brink of war.

Fig 25. *Old Boys. Back row left George; back row middle TM; second row second from right William.*

EPILOGUE

Those who have read this story might be interested to learn what became of William, George and me.

I was sixteen and a half when war broke out, too young to join up. I worked and lodged in Cambridge, where I met a couple who more or less adopted me, and gave me what I craved: a secure, loving family. As soon as I was old enough, I volunteered for the Navy and saw a bit of the world. I served a short spell on Russian convoys, went to the USA to commission a newly-built ship, spent two years convoying off the West African coast, and six months on the royal yacht *Victoria and Albert*. I was demobbed in 1946.

In 1948 I married Kathleen, and had the joy of a home of my own. Kathleen died in 1963 leaving me with our seven-and-a-half-year-old son, Mark. Three years later I met Lillian, with whom I shared twenty-seven years of love and happiness.

For two-and-a-half decades I worked at the University Arms Hotel in Cambridge. I was contented enough to begin with, but Lillian, who could read me like a book, realised, without my saying anything, that I was becoming increasingly disillusioned and needed a change. It was she who heard of the assistant butler's post at Peterhouse, and who persuaded – or should I say compelled? – me to apply. I was lucky enough to be successful, and, at the same time, she was taken on as housekeeper in one of the college houses. Thus we both became part of Peterhouse, and it proved a most rewarding move. Lillian got on wonderfully with the undergraduates in her charge, creating for them what amounted to a home from home, while still looking after our own two sons. For my part, I quickly realised I'd found my true vocation. I rose to become college butler, and finally Master's butler. I have retired now, but I live in a college house, and am happy to be called in to help with functions on special occasions.

A Cambridge college is a world of its own, and I have been lucky enough to serve and enjoy the friendship of a number of brilliant and distinguished people. I would single out, the late Sir Herbert Butterfield, the Rev. Professor Sir Henry Chadwick, Lord Dacre, Professor Jacques Heyman, Sir Aaron Klug OM, FRS, Dr Max Perutz OM, Mr Michael Portillo, and the late Professor Edward Shils, an American, who used to spend half the year in Cambridge and half in Chicago.

William left the orphanage in 1940, and later joined the Navy. After he was demobbed he got a job as a baker, and then moved up to Yorkshire, married and had two children. I am sad to say that he lost a brave fight against cancer in August this year.

George left the orphanage in 1942, and he, too, went into the Navy. He became a long-distance lorry driver, and nearly lost his life in a road accident. Happily he recovered completely, and he lives in a village in Cambridgeshire. He has three children and two stepchildren.

The differences in our characters, already noticeable when we were boys, were, perhaps, accentuated by age and experience; but I am happy to say that we always remained in close touch, and that there was a strong bond between us.

Fig 26. *William left the orphanage in 1940 and later joined the Navy.*

I lost contact with my friend Hoska after we both left the orphanage. I believe he joined the Army and did not survive the War.